Business Internships

D1268303

Michael P. Griffin
Charlton College of Business
University of Massachusetts Dartmouth

Swansea Publishing Group

Swansea, Massachusetts

Published by Swansea Publishing Group
808 Wood Street
Swansea, Massachusetts

ISBN: 978-1-4357-9016-2

Bulk orders available upon request. Digital versions of book are also available. Email: mgriffin@umassd.edu

To my family: My wife Nan, and my children Brendan, Kate, Allison, and Trevor.

Introduction

COLLEGE STUDENTS HAVE BEEN INTERNING for more than 100 years. Back before the turn of the 20th century, schools like the University of Cincinnati and MIT were utilizing co-operative education so students could gain real world experience before they hit the job market. Northeastern University in Boston, Massachusetts has long been known for its internship and co-op programs; a major selling point of their recruiting efforts.

At the Charlton College of Business of the University of Massachusetts Dartmouth where I am the internship director, we have been offering internships-for-credit for several years and have worked with both employers and students to develop powerful partnerships yielding great benefits to both parties.

Employers are keen on internships and why not? Research shows that organizations with established internship programs report higher retention rates among employees who started as interns. Many intern employers use internships as a means to recruit future managers.

Parents and students are fond of internships. The most frequent question at our college open houses is: "Do you have an internship program?" Students overwhelmingly view internships as critical to their career plans and many students factor in the possibility of internships when they select a business school. Parents like to think that once their child is established at college, the next logical step will be getting real world experience through an internship and networking with professionals who can offer career advice and connections.

At the Charlton College of Business, our students are interning with a variety of companies including manufacturers, CPA firms, retailers, museums, nonprofit organizations, and companies in the restaurant and hospitality fields. Many of our employers are located on the south coast of Massachusetts and on Cape Cod but in the summer, many of our students return to their home towns and secure exciting internships. Others might travel many miles to places like Boston, New York City or London to gain real world work experience with hopes of coming back to our region a bit transformed.

We have had students working for well- known companies such as Putnam Investments, Fidelity Investments, State Street Corporation, KPMG, Raytheon, Nestle Waters (Poland Springs) and Johnson and Johnson. Summer internships allow students to immerse themselves in the experience without the distraction of a heavy course load. We have accounting students working in the summer for the big accounting firms, such as PricewaterhouseCoopers and students completing sports oriented internships with the Boston Bruins, the Kraft Sports Group (New England Patriots), Pawtucket Red Sox (the triple A affiliate of the Boston Red Sox) and the National Baseball Hall of Fame in Cooperstown, New York.

Recruiting for full-time employment can begin with a good internship. Interning allows for an extended and low-risk tryout. So much more can be learned about a job candidate during a 10 or 15 week internship than in a half hour interview. As the baby boom generation retires, companies are ramping up their internship programs as a tool to recruit the next generation of workers and fill critical skill gaps.

A survey by Veritude reported in *Workforce Data Insights* found that an overwhelming majority of respondents (83 percent) believe that internship programs are either important or very important for their companies' long term workforce development. Internships are recruiting tools – there can be no doubt about that. According to a survey conducted by the National Association of Colleges and Employers (NACE), 98 percent of companies that have internship programs reported using them as a recruitment tool for full-time employees.

Internships come in all shapes and sizes. Our students work for large and small firms, for profit enterprises and nonprofit entities. Some of the largest employers in our region are nonprofit organizations who are extremely interested in tapping into the talent of our undergraduate business program. We also have students doing business internships in distant places such as Washington D.C. through the Washington Center, Orlando, Florida at Disney and at Cooperstown Dream Park in upstate New York. We have had interns in Ireland, Germany, and France.

There is no one place to look for internships, some of the best programs might be outside your geographic regions and therefore travel or temporary relocation (such as in the summer) might be required. Some of the best situations to learn about a business might be found in a small business internships or a nonprofit organization where an intern might have to master many tasks in a less specialized and more generalist role.

As I have worked with our talented business students, I have learned a great deal about internships, and I have come to value internships immensely (much more than I did before I became director of our internship program). Therefore, I decided it was important to educate others about internships and to share the information and lessons I have learned. I hope this book provides you with some valuable insights.

The biggest advantage that I see for the student is that the right internships can truly transform. Upon completing successful internships, many students have told me that they believe it was one of the most rewarding experiences of their lives. My hope is that this book can help students increase the odds of completing a great business internship. I also hope this book can be used to guide faculty who might be new to internships and provide professors with a map to direct students through an excellent internship process.

Michael P. Griffin
Charlton College of Business
University of Massachusetts Dartmouth
July 2011

Contents

Chapter 1

The Importance of an Internship

At the Charlton College of Business, where I am the internship program director, we believe that an internship is important if not critical in helping a student develop into a business professional. Although we don't require it, we believe that just about every student should complete an internship before they graduate.

At our college and at many others across the U.S. and the globe, internships allow students to earn academic credit by combining significant work experience with academic study. These opportunities recognize the value of work experience and the critical mental reflection of that work, as an important part of learning. The idea is that book knowledge is not enough and that a practicum – a supervised practical application of a previously or concurrently studied theory – is key to the development of a professional. This is true in other professional schools such as nursing, education, law, and engineering. If by our encouragement we can help students get out into the field to do some practical learning – then we have achieved an important victory. And we stand ready to help assure quality learning engagements. But let's not get ahead of ourselves, before we go on let's make sure we understand the meaning of the word "internship", a terms sometimes too loosely defined.

What is an Internship?

What is an internship? It can mean different things to different people. Some people believe any part-time job is an internship or that any type of unpaid work performed by a college student is an internship. That is not how we define internship.

The United States Department of Labor (DOL), the federal agency that is charged with preparing the American workforce for new and better jobs, has its own definition of an internship. That definition has taken on a more important meaning recently as the DOL has raised concerns about unpaid internships that are clearly disguised jobs without pay.

The DOL believes, as one lawyer recently paraphrased, that "an internship supplements classroom study with on-the-job study and that the primary result is a more learned or skilled student – not a saleable work product." A more learned or more skilled student is the primary goal of an internship at my college. When I find an internship provider who understands that goal, then half of the battle is won.

The priority with an internship should be on learning and connecting the student's classroom studies to the real world. For example, an accounting student who learns how to prepare tax returns is learning how to apply the knowledge and skills learned in an income tax course to a real world practice. My accounting students have worked in CPA firms preparing tax returns and for a nonprofit organization that aids the poor in preparation of their tax returns through the VITA program. VITA stands for Volunteer Income Tax Assistance – a U.S. federal program sponsored by the IRS and others, such as Wal-Mart. VITA helps low income tax payers take advantage of the earned income credit (EIC). VITA puts millions of dollars back into the hands of disadvantaged citizens and therefore also puts money back into local economies. By participating in our VITA internships, students learn the practical application of the IRS code while seeing the impact of helping folks maximize their tax refunds.

In New Bedford, Massachusetts, a city located just a few miles from our campus, a nonprofit organization named the Community Economic Development Center of Southeastern Massachusetts, administers the VITA program. They also train our students on how to interview taxpayers, collect data, and prepare the tax return. Each of those tasks - interviewing, collecting data and preparing real tax returns cannot be learned in the classroom. Therein lays the beauty of an internship.

The VITA student interns also help with the daily running of the nonprofit organization with duties beyond the income tax preparation service and draw upon communication and interpersonal skills – something I believe many accounting majors need to master to become true professionals.

When employers call me and want to talk about establishing an internship, I make it clear that at our college, we work with a clear definition of an internship and I want to make it apparent that they need to adopt the same definition. Here's what we expect:

> *An internship is an arrangement whereby an employer provides supervised training and on-the-job learning experiences (at a professional level) consisting of at least 9 hours a week on the job and 1 hour per week participating in an internship course for a total of 150 hours per semester.*

Other business schools may have slightly different definitions of internships but I believe ours is quite clear: you must work in the field and complete our internship course to receive credit.

Albert Einstein once said: "The only source of knowledge is experience." I wouldn't go that far because as an academic I truly believe that much can be learned from reading and reflective writing, but I do believe that a certain type of knowledge for future professionals is gained through real world experience in the bright light of a quality classroom education.

We require that our internships run concurrent with the semester and we require that students who earn credit via an internship do it by completing an internship course. The National Association of Colleges and Employers has found that only 28 percent of colleges associate classroom experience with academic credit for internships, while 25 percent do not require any kind of written assignments, 15 percent do not require any faculty supervision, and 6 percent require nothing at all.

Another requirement that I believe is essential to a solid college internship program is that we will not grant credit for past experiences. That's another misconception that both students and parents sometimes have. For example, a student cannot earn credits retroactively in the fall semester based on hours worked in the previous summer. We require that as the student is carrying out the responsibilities of their internship - that they complete an online internship course with work journals, discussions, and writing assignments that cause the student to reflect and report on and carefully document on the internship experience.

We enforce the concurrent stipulation (take the course while completing the internship) because we want to be able to monitor what is happening. We hope to witness and assess learning as it is happening in the field. That is a control feature of our program: a way of monitoring quality as the internship is being played out.

Then there is the rigor of learning. Internships without sufficient rigor of learning are not valuable and most smart students recognize a soft internship when they see it. A proposed internship without a true learning element is a "light-weight" experience and I won't approve it for credit unless it is restructured into something that will help the student meet important learning objectives.

With internships, professors and administrators should not be in the business of granting credit just for jobs or employment. There should be evidence of learning as the internship is played out by building into internship classes, activities, and outputs such as goal setting, periodic reporting (through discussions, papers and journals), evaluations, interviews, term paper writing and site visits (that's usually my responsibility as internship professor). What are even better than solid learning activities and outputs required by an internship course are activities and outputs required by the internship provider.

A required internship course or a faculty sponsorship that helps monitor progress and assures a high quality experience is critical and very beneficial to the student. Accountability is one of the keys to an excellent internship and students should not shy away from accountability; they should look for it and embrace it in an internship.

The Front-End Quality Control of an Internship

Just as in total quality management of a process such as manufacturing, we try to exert quality control on the front end of the process of all our internships. We look to see that an internship requires more learning activities than a regular part-time job. We look to employers to demonstrate that their internship program involves enough rigorous learning to justify three college credits, which we award as a business elective to any student who passes the internship course and fulfills the minimum work hour's requirement.

The work experience must provide the student with a professional-level learning experience and should consist of both supervised training and on-the-job learning activities. A professional work environment is a key factor: one that values learning, requires a mastery of some body of knowledge, and is directed by managers and executives who are experienced.

If you are a student looking at accepting an internship offer from an organization, you should understand that an upfront quality review is necessary. Your judgment of quality - your due diligence should begin with the work environment. I suggest to students that they carefully judge the prospects of a professional work environment. If you have any trepidation about that, then back off and look at other opportunities because without a great environment – one controlled by experienced professionals who believe in the internship experience - then internship is doomed to fail.

Getting feedback from other students who have completed internships is very valuable. Just as students ask around about professors or visit the rate-your-professor type of web sites, prospective interns should ask around about internship providers. One web site, InternshipKing.com (www.internshipking.com/) offers students the chance to rate their internships online. The downside of a service like InternshipKing is that it carries feedback on mostly nationally recognized internships like Nike and Apple, but if you are interested in some of the big programs, visit InternshipKing.com and check out the reviews.

Be Careful - Eyes Wide Open

Sometimes the professional work environment requirement can be challenged to the point of absurdity. A few years back, a student contacted me about an internship opportunity in the MIS field. She told me that she had an interview with a "networking company". I assumed this was a firm that provided computer networks or perhaps installed home networks for people who worked in a home office.

A few days after the "interview", the student called me with some concerns. She said that the entrepreneur who ran the networking company, met her at his office at a local mall. I said: "I didn't realize that the mall rented office space." She said: "It doesn't." She went on to tell me that the "office" was at the local Panera Bread – a coffee/bakery/sandwich shop in the North Dartmouth mall. I love Panera Bread – it's a great place to have a coffee and to meet people. I even stop there sometimes to answer my email and surf the web, but I certainly don't want my students doing internships for a guy who runs his "networking business" from a coffee shop.

I have had other alarming revelations about places of business like marketing interns that found out after accepting the internship, that they were required to go door to door selling, and rarely saw the inside of the marketing company's office. I have had other students tell me that they will be working from their dorms as the company doesn't have enough space for them. If the company cannot provide a work space and a place from which the intern's work will be reviewed and supervised and from which training and learning can happen, then that is not an internship that I want my students to complete. I want my students to stay away from that kind of "internship" experience and focus on finding one that has all the ingredients of a professional work environment including:

- Managers and mentors who value learning.

- Managers and mentors who will provide supervision.

- Good logistics - a place for the interns to work with all they need to do the work.

- A pleasant atmosphere with people who are accepting, polite, pleasant, and respectful.

- Challenging - helping students achieve goals.

Avoid Internship Farce

A farce is an often humorous improbable and absurd situation. A farce can make for good TV, movie scenes, or acts of a play. Some internships can be farces and there is nothing funny about wasting your time interning in an absurd situation where most of your time is spent doing menial or routine tasks or sitting idle.

The best type of internship requires the student to perform such skills as researching, organizing, writing, and managing projects. Internships that require lots of photocopying, filing, and or data entry are not meaty enough to challenge you, to help you learn, and to transform you into a business professional. Internships that offer you lots of idle time, where you surf the web or do your homework are not truly internships. They also don't contain enough learning to truly justify college credit.

In a very funny (farcical) Seinfeld episode called *The Voice* (which first aired in October of 1997), Jerry's oddball neighbor Cosmo Kramer, hires an intern from New York University (NYU) to help him run his fledgling company named Kramerica Industries – which Kramer runs out of his apartment.

As you can imagine, it is a very questionable internship. In the episode, Darren, the-intern, performs mundane activities such as setting appointments for Kramer – such as coffee at the local diner with Jerry and taking notes while Kramer and Jerry converse over coffee.

When Jerry first meets Darren, he asks Kramer about the internship. Here's the dialog.

> KRAMER: Well, apparently NYU is very enthusiastic about their students getting some real world corporate experience.

> JERRY: But you only provide fantasy world corporate experience.

And Jerry was right; the internship at Kramerica Industries was nothing more than a fantasy. Eventually, Kramer, as the intern sponsor, must meet with the student's Dean at NYU to discuss Darren's internship. Here's the hilarious dialog from the scene at NYU.

Scene: Meeting between Kramer and Dean Jones at New York University

KRAMER: Dean Jones, you wanting to talk to me?

DEAN JONES: I've been reviewing Darren's internship journal. Doing laundry…

KRAMER: …Yeah.

DEAN JONES: …Mending chicken wire, hi-tea with a Mr. Newman.

KRAMER: I know it sounds pretty glamorous, but it's business as usual at Kramerica.

DEAN JONES: As far as I can tell your entire enterprise is no more than a solitary man with a messy apartment which may or may not contain a chicken.

KRAMER: And with Darren's help, we'll get that chicken.

DEAN JONES: I'm sorry, but we can't allow Darren to continue working with you.

KRAMER: Well, I have to say this seems capricious and arbitrary.

DEAN JONES: Your fly is open.

Source: Seinfeld episode called *The Voice* (which first aired in October of 1997)

To Kramer, the Dean's demand that the internship be terminated seems "capricious and arbitrary", but any application of common sense should tell us that the internship was a farce and should be ended. The last thing I want to learn is that a student's internship turned out to be a light-weight experience. Colleges and universities must work to put standards in place and develop curriculum that helps assure a quality internship experience. Students must also demand that companies challenge them and that mentors teach them the practical applications of book theory that will lead to a successful career.

Reasons Why Students Complete Internships

Are you sold on the idea of an internship? If you are in an internship and are trying to earn academic credit then obviously the answer to my question is – "Yes I am sold on the idea." If you are reading this book as preparation to begin the process of landing a great internship, but are not quite sure of yourself then I suggest you examine the reasons why students are interested in internships and why many employers see the value of internships. If you are an employer who is looking at offering internships, think of the win/win. An internship can help your organization in a number of ways, but have you thought about what attracts students to internships?

I am always asking students to email me to tell me why they want to do an internship. Here are some of the common responses from college students to that question:

- To gain hands-on work experience

- To learn new skills

- To become better prepared to be employed in a specific field

- To make professional contacts for future networking

- To be given a realistic preview of the work world

- To explore a new organization or industry

- To earn money

- To receive a full-time job offer from an employer

- To receive college credit

- To fulfill degree requirements

- To take part in community service

Each item in the above list is a great reason to do an internship. Employers also provide motivations when they repeatedly explain that a good GPA, a track record of part-time and summer jobs, and participation in student activities and organizations are not enough to help students land a good full-time job. In today's competitive job market, the students with career-related work experience (internship) are the students who get the best interviews and job offers.

More and more job postings on services such as Monster.com or Indeed.com mention the expectations or in some cases, the requirement of internship experiences. Students who have completed internships are simply more employment-ready than the majority of students who have not completed an internship.

While any one of the above reasons to do an internship is compelling, I advise students to adopt a set of internship goals: objectives to be accomplished during the semester-long journey of an internship. I suggest that these goals be documented – set down in writing so they can become guiding lights. I also suggest that a final term paper for the internship include these goals, how they were accomplished, or why they were not seen through to fruition. I try to drive home the idea that the best type of internship is one that is goal-driven.

Goals of Business Internships

In a best-case scenario, each student intern should develop custom goals for their internship. For example, a young lady told me that one of her goals was to combine two of her favorite things (marketing and baseball) into an internship. She applied for a marketing internship with the Pawtucket Red Sox at McCoy Stadium in Pawtucket, Rhode Island. The Paw Sox are the triple A (AAA) affiliate of the Boston Red Sox. As the AAA farm club, the organization is very aggressive about marketing the games and publicizing such events as bobble-head night or rehab stints by major league players coming off the disabled list. My student helped with the marketing of events, community outreach, and ticket sales. She loved the experience and it helped her reach some career goals.

What I usually suggest to students is that there are some generic goals that can be used as a starting point for just about any internship, and that some of these generic goals (see the list below this paragraph) might need to be customized for their own situations. For example, a neighbor of mine was an excellent accounting student at the University of Massachusetts Dartmouth. I had her in several classes and she was a hardworking and bright student. However, she wasn't sure whether she wanted to go into public accounting or start out as a staff accountant or an internal auditor for a corporation. She landed an internship with a regional accounting firm in Providence, Rhode Island and loved the experience so much that she accepted an offer to work full-time for the firm. One of her goals was to test the possible career path of public accounting and she accomplished it in a brilliant way with the best possible outcome - a full-time job offer!

Generic goals that you can use as an intern (or customize a bit for your specific situation) include:

- Applying business theory to actual working situations.
- Gaining new knowledge by performing tasks, working on projects, and completing other on-the-job learning experiences related to a business discipline.
- Gaining a greater degree of self-direction in the learning process.
- Testing a tentative career choice.
- Allowing an employer to test you (keep in mind that internships are an effective recruiting tool – a way to "screen out" potential full-time employees).

At our business college, we are always looking for new internship employers who are willing to help students achieve their goals. I market our program along the lines of those generic goals listed above. I tell employers that no matter what their pressing concerns might be – a helping hand around a busy office, selling and marketing talent, web site design and maintenance, tax return preparation, etc. they must keep a watchful eye towards meeting the learning goals of the student. I want to see activities that help the student strive towards the goals and I want to see periodic written reflections of that progress towards the goals. I require written assignments along those lines and the preparation of simple work journals that document and describe the work performed, the tasks and projects completed, and the training acquired along the way (which is usually a 15 week semester in the fall and spring, and a 10 week semester in the summer.)

A vision of what you want students to get out of their internships needs to be a driving force. Three parties to the internship need this vision: the student, the faculty member, and the internship supervisor/mentor.

At the Charlton College of Business we want our students to have the opportunity before they graduate to apply theory to actual working situations. We want employers/internship providers who will offer chances for our students to learn new knowledge - perhaps allow for some self-directed learning and discovery - and who are not only interested in recruiting our talented undergraduates but also allowing our students to test the waters.

One big benefit of an internship is what I call career path validation: trying to figure out if this is what you want to do for a career. How will you ever learn if you are on the right path if you don't complete an internship? You could wait to start your career with a full-time position but if possible, take a walk down the first part of a career path by landing an internship.

If you are a business student looking at internships (and especially if you land an internship) before you go too far, ask yourself these two questions:

- *Will I gain new knowledge by performing on-the-job tasks of an internship?*

- *With the internship, will I be working on projects and completing other on-the-job learning experiences that are related to a business discipline?*

If the answers to these questions are YES, then you might be on the right track. You owe it to yourself to answer these questions.

Mentoring and Coaching

We want our students to have the opportunity to be mentored and coached by experienced managers and executives but we also want them to have a chance at self-directed learning and discovery. We hope for situations that allow our interns to dig deeper into areas of career-interest and to explore career paths more thoroughly than they might in their typical course assignments.

Although I set a syllabus and require certain assignments, there are no limits to what can be learned in a good internship. I am always surprised, each semester, by the revelations made by interns in their term papers: a reflective final assignment required of all our interns.

Our student interns must write a 10 page term paper that documents the entire internship experience. The paper is one way to demonstrate what has been accomplished via the internship and to demonstrate what they have learned. The goals that are achieved and the things students learn about the company and themselves are often pleasant surprises for me. It's not that I am surprised that the students have had good experiences as I have come to learn that so many internship providers do a great service for our students. It is just that when I read the papers I often think – "Well I never expected that, but I am glad and impressed that it happened."

Mentorship is a huge part of internships and it is the mentor who can provide lots of valuable learning experiences for the intern. As you contemplate a particular internship opportunity, discover if you will be supervised by a well educated and experienced mentor and think about what you might gain from that relationship. What learning have they completed and what wisdom have they accumulated that can be passed on to you? What can you learn – both good and bad – from their example?

One of our interns described a situation handled by her boss who was rude and unethical. In no way did this boss recognize the dignity of the individual and the incident bordered on cruel and heartless workplace behavior. My student correctly noted in her final paper that someday when she is a manager, she will work to uphold the dignity of the person no matter how difficult the situation. That is a type of professional empathy that can only come from witnessing this type of workplace behavior and reflecting upon it with the conclusion being a fine lesson learned.

An internship is often your first exposure to a professional work environment. Students often learn how to work and conduct themselves in a traditional business setting – one that that they probably have not been in before. They experience what is expected in the real world such as strict punctuality, reliability, adherence to the tasks at hand, impeccable manners, and in some cases, dress codes. These are often new but valuable lessons to the inexperienced student, but those experiences just don't happen. Supervisors and mentors must introduce these concepts to the raw recruits. Mentoring and coaching interns is the sole responsibility of the employer and that duty must be taken very seriously as it provides the way to add-value to the experience. We have been so very fortunate at the Charlton College. A vast majority of our internship providers are excellent mentors and coaches for our student interns.

The Conversion Process

In a competitive job market internships can set you apart. They provide a great résumé item and make you more desirable to potential employers. In the best of internships, a conversion takes place. A student who is "wet behind the ears" learns over the course of 15 weeks to get to work on time, meet expectations, act professionally, become engaged in the work of the organization, and adhere to work policies. Employers value internships partly because of the conversion process. They (employers) see that much internship have resulted in activities that transform the intern into a valuable employee.

However, related to a previous point about the importance of the coaching and mentoring of students is the idea that the conversion process happens because of good supervisors, a fact that future employers will recognize when they see it. Seeing that you have already worked in a professional environment, a potential employer will conclude that you have some experience and knowledge and that some "fit and finish" work has already been completed. You will be "on your way" because of the internship conversion process. This will help you move faster along the learning curve, a slope always evident in the early days of a career. The assumption will be that you will provide value sooner than another job candidate who did not complete an internship. This is something all serious minded entry-level employees want – a chance to be a contributor – sooner rather than later.

Starting the Walk down a Career Path

Many first and second year students (and often third and fourth year students) have no clear career plans. They can't arrive at any real career clarity when looking forward. The answer to the classic interview question: "Where do you see yourself in 5 years?" is as confusing and hazy to many students as "What is the meaning of life?" I have often thought: "What can be done to clear your career vision so you can see where you are going?" and "How do you begin to take a walk down your chosen career path?"

Since it is quite difficult for anyone to define what job or which precise career path will make you happy and successful, one strategy is to experiment – to test the waters and see what happens. I think that you will agree that so much learning comes from trial-and-error and although experiments do tend to be an inefficient and time consuming way of learning, there is often no better way to proceed than with the discovery of experimentation.

So it is true that career clarification may come from the internship testing ground. Some people believe you should not leave school without an internship, without a chance to experiment in the laboratory called the workplace. When you complete an internship, the hope is that you will have a better idea of what you want to do for a living – at least when you first graduate from school.

Career clarity through an internship may also have a much unexpected but equally as valuable outcome. You may finish your internship and decide that your career path is headed in the wrong direction. You may learn that some adjustments need to be made in your pursuit of a career. That too is valuable; so if you have to go back to the drawing board or visit with a career counselor after your internship experience to identify a possible new career path, don't be disappointed. Many of us need to test and re-test our plans.

I never completed an internship when I was in school, but I always held a job during college. For all of my years in undergraduate school and part of grad school I worked for Sears, a large retailer. I performed a variety of jobs including working in the receiving department, men's clothing, carpeting, and floor covering, and I even did stints in the TV and stereo, automotive and sporting goods departments. Some of those assignments were fun and I loved the variety. I actually could see myself becoming a manager of a few of those departments. I liked the fact that I got to meet people, did not have to sit behind a desk, and was always busy. I was fascinated by some of the products and services we sold. To this day, I use some of my experiences from retailing when I try to illuminate accounting principles in my classes. I am an accounting professor and all of my work experiences, including those as a part-timer at Sears, help me with my current job.

When I went to graduate school for my MBA, I also worked as a substitute teacher as I could work until mid afternoon and then go to my classes in the late afternoon and evening. It was a perfect match and I loved the job immensely; the day went by fast, I was dealing with young people, which I enjoyed, and in many ways, was my own boss.

When I landed my first full-time job after college, I enjoyed some of the work in the financial services field (banking and personal financial planning), but I didn't enjoy sitting behind a desk all day. There also wasn't enough variety for me. I would think about how happy I was working in retailing at Sears, how each day was different and I would especially think about all the satisfaction I had as a substitute teacher helping students. Those memories made me gravitate towards teaching at the college level. I found my way to a happy career because of my part-time job experiences and coming to terms with what I liked and disliked about jobs. I changed direction and became a college professor and other than the fact that I probably would have made much more money in the private sector, I have never looked back because I have been happy with my career in academia.

Can an internship lead to happiness in your career? I think so. If your internship experience presents more dissatisfaction than joy, isn't it best to make a change in direction rather than committing to something that will make you unhappy? There are few things worse than being stuck in an uninspiring career or a job you hate. Life is too short to dread going to work each day. Ideally, use your "internship experience" to find yourself or find a suitable career path and even if that is not accomplished think about a second internship and additional research into other possible fulfilling career paths.

The Road Not Taken

When I think about career path choices and finding your way in life, I can't help think about Robert Frost's poem entitled: *The Road Not Taken*. My thoughts hearken back to the last few lines of the poem:

Two roads diverged in a wood, and I—
I took the one less traveled by,
And that has made all the difference[1]

Sometimes the "road not taken" is the best move you can make with a career. An internship may guide you away from your first choice for a career and there is nothing wrong with that. The key thing is that you should make progress towards a career that will make you happy and provide you with a good standard of living. I really believe that an internship is a good first step.

Why Students Don't Do an Internship

Even though there are terrific reasons why students choose to do an internship and even though there are very valuable goals to be achieved by completing a semester-long internship, not every student completes an internship during their undergraduate days. One reason is that internships can be in short supply and like full-time jobs, they are not always easy to find. Students visit with me, email me, and call me on the phone almost weekly admitting their frustration with finding good leads for an internship that will meet their needs. Like many colleges, we do not place students in internships, so students must work hard, perhaps with the assistance of a career development counselor, to find solid leads on internship openings. It's not easy to find a good internship and some students give up. Later on in this text I will give tips on how to land an internship, and I truly believe if you work smart and have persistence you will find a good internship, but keep in mind it doesn't always happen. Many factors can come into play and some may be beyond your control. Difficult economic times and other constraining factors impact the supply of good internships.

There are other reasons why students may choose not to pursue an internship. Students talk to me all the time about how they have

---

[1] Frost, Robert. *Mountain Interval.* New York: Henry Holt and Company, 1920.

reservations about being able to balance a course load with an internship. Some students simply believe they do not have the time to work 10-15 hours per week because they have too much school work. This is a legitimate concern and in many ways, a very mature and priority driven conclusion. As I mentioned previously, as an undergraduate I never had an official internship, but I believe I gained great value from my part-time jobs. Students sometimes opt for shorter-term experiences as almost surrogates for internships - experiences such as job shadowing, practical projects in the field as part of class assignments, civic engagement projects, and other volunteer efforts. Another popular angle is something called externships.

An externship is an experiential learning opportunity, similar to an internship, offered by educational institutions to give students short practical experiences in their field of study. The duration of the engagement is much shorter - often about 1/3 the time of an internship. Sometimes these experiences are documented on the college transcript as noncredit experiences while some schools will award 1 credit for an externship. Perhaps a series of externships can provide the feedback and experience you need to bring you career clarity.

Time Management and the Internship

Many students have been able to carry off the delicate balancing act of going to school full-time and working at an internship. Those students that thrive academically and on the job during an internship seem to master time management. Time management principles can help a student manage both the demands of a heavy course load and an internship and I suggest to students a wonderful video on YouTube by the late Dr. Randy Pausch, the author of the best-selling book: *The Last Lecture*. Pausch, a Carnegie Mellon Professor, gave a lecture on Time Management at the University of Virginia in November 2007 and I require that all my interns watch it. You should be able to find it on Youtube.com - it is awesome.

Time is a big problem for college student athletes and other students who have committed to extracurricular activities and say: "I do not have time because I am involved in too many school activities." Again, I advise students to look to summer internships as a solution to the lack of time problem. For example, a college baseball player that I know wanted to do an internship but waited till the summer time when he landed a gig with WEEI Boston, one of the top sports talk radio stations in the United States. We not only encourage summer internships but we also award credit for such internships through our web-based internship course.

Students also get discouraged in their internship hunt and tell me that there are no interesting internships close enough to where they live. This is a legitimate concern for some students. For example, our region – the south coast of Massachusetts – is roughly 60 miles from Boston and 30 miles from Providence, RI. There are very few large manufacturers close by where an operations management major could do an internship. Travel times of over an hour might be common to work at such an internship and that amount of travel within a week full of course demands and school activities might simply burn you out.

Some of our students have found that the summer is a good time to do a "far-away" internship and have travel from the Providence, RI/New Bedford area to places like New York City, Cooperstown, NY, San Diego, California, Washington DC, Dublin, Ireland, and London, England in an attempt to land an internship that meets their specific goals.

For two straight summers, two of my students completed internships in Cooperstown, New York – one at the National Baseball Hall of Fame and another at Cooperstown Dream Parks - a massive and amazing youth baseball complex that host over 90 teams each week during the summer for tournaments. Cooperstown is several hours from our campus but these were unique experiences that matched well with the interests and goals of these two students.

National averages show that most internships are done in the summer (almost 60%) with the remaining 40% spread almost evenly between fall and spring semesters.[2] At our college, our busiest internship semester is the spring, partly because we have many accounting students who work for CPA firms during the tax season. Our second busiest season is in the summer.

Another factor that works against internships is the need for students to earn money. At the University of Massachusetts Dartmouth, we have many students who need to be paid to work; otherwise they cannot make ends meet. It is as simple as that. Many of our students must earn wages from part-time jobs to pay for tuition, fees, books, a laptop, transportation and other living expenses, and then do not have time to also put in 10 to 15 hours a week in an unpaid internship.

Sometimes we are successful in finding internships that pay an adequate hourly wage and so this hurdle is obliterated. The pay versus nonpaid internship quandary remains a dilemma for many and is not always easily

---

[2] Reported by Intern Bridge, Inc. June 2009 based on a national survey. Intern Bridge is responsible for the nation's largest annual internship research projects. Their web site is www.internbridge.com/index.htm

managed. Even some of our local business people balk at the idea of paying interns, but I tell them that the best candidates can probably find a paid position.

When students ask for my advice on this topic, I consistently tell them that they must do whatever is best for their studies, and if that means working in a paid job (not an internship) to continue to afford school and basic living expenses, it is a no brainer. I advise them to keep working the paying job and maybe another semester will be a better time for an internship or perhaps the best of both worlds will merge – they will find an internship that pays. The two goals of learning and earning do not have to be mutually exclusive. We have had many students earning some good money in paid internships.

Many of our students give up too fast. They do a few quick searches on the Internet, send out some letters and résumés, make a few inquiries, and even go as far as applying for an internship or two, but when they are not offered a position, they give up. Rewards come to those who keep looking, keep applying, and persevere. Don't get discouraged if your first several attempts at landing an internship don't work out.

Checklist of First Steps

✓ Understand the definition of an internship

✓ Set personal goals

✓ Find a professional environment to target for an internship

✓ Start thinking of a plan to help you "test the waters"

✓ Be persistent in you search, it could take time

Chapter 2

Planning for an Internship

IT IS NEVER TOO EARLY to start thinking about an internship. In fact, I tell high school students to start thinking about internships immediately. Some high school students complete an internship before they graduate from high school. Such a practice is common in vocational high schools. For example, I visited a local technical high school and learned that hundreds of their students complete internships each year.

For our college business students, I recommend that they plan early but wait till they complete their sophomore year before they participate in an internship. There are three reasons for this:

1. After the sophomore year, students will have some introductory business courses completed which will make it easier to see the connections between business principles and real world work. With some business knowledge in place, richer and deeper reflections on business activities are possible. Some things really do get better with time and such is the case when trying to apply book-learned knowledge to real world situations.

2. Our college policy restricts the granting of internship credit to only juniors and seniors; partly because of reason number 1 above.

3. Our internships are business electives and most of our students don't have the chance to take business electives until sometime in their last two years.

Before your junior year, start thinking about the type of internship you would like to do. I often suggest that college students start learning about internships in their freshman year. Landing a great internship should be a long-term goal – not something you start working on in your senior year. One reason for this is that many internship opportunities come about from the professional contacts you make along the way. For example, some of our accounting majors join the college accounting club in their freshman or sophomore years. As a result, they meet accounting firm partners, sole practitioners, accounting managers, controllers, and finance executives who visit us as speakers or who mingle with our students at college sponsored events. It is from those contacts that accounting majors land internships.

Experienced professionals are a source for great internships – especially experienced professionals who are alumni of the school. We have alumni at large corporations, such as Textron – an international conglomerate located in Providence, RI. Those alums have been terrific advocates for internships and have helped several of our students move into excellent internships at company headquarters. We have also had great advocates and alumni mentors at Hasbro, the large toy maker located in Pawtucket, RI and at numerous accounting firms in our region. Successful alumni are the best source of quality internships.

The lesson is that it is never too early to start "networking" with professionals who could possibly someday offer you an internship and eventually – a job. Seek out people who have been out of school a few years and are established in their companies and better yet, graduated from your school. Those are the people who can help you land a great internship.

Making Academics More Meaningful

Thinking and planning early in your academic career for an internship helps you gain more from your studies. I tell students that if they decide that they want to do an internship with a CPA firm, it is very likely that they will need to know something about income taxes as many firms place interns in their tax departments during tax season.

Perhaps voluntary involvement in a program like VITA (a community service program whereby college students help low income taxpayers with tax return preparation) would not only be an impressive résumé item but would provide some excellent background and training for a tax internship.

The best type of internship is one that is clearly aligned with your major. For example, many accounting majors intern at CPA firms or in the internal audit department of a bank. Marketing interns work for advertising agencies or help registered representatives market various financial services and products. MIS majors intern in IT departments or help small companies manage their web sites and ecommerce functions.

An internship that is carefully aligned with your major has many advantages. It allows you to see in action what you have read about and discussed in class. Such internships may also pave the way to a full-time job offer at the same firm or at another company. However, you may also consider doing an internship that is outside of your major. At the Charlton College of Business, our students can use an internship to fulfill one of their business electives and that allows opportunity to work in an internship different from a chosen major. For example, I have had accounting majors who are interested in investment advisory services or personal financial planning and have taken internships with Northwestern Mutual, a company that has been recognized for 13 straight years as a top internship provider.

Internships in an area different from the focus of a student's major can help that student acquire a depth and breadth of knowledge that could be very valuable in a career. A finance major might complete a marketing internship to increase knowledge, skills, and abilities related to promotion, sales, and marketing: valuable combinations for future work in the financial services industry. Sometimes marketing majors perform IT internships, especially in the area of web development and ecommerce as a nice complement to their major.

There are many possibilities as business and nonprofit managers must perform cross functional tasks everyday and so it makes sense to complete an internship that allows you to cross over into a business discipline outside of your specific major. The real world isn't always organized neatly like the business majors of a college (functionality) or the departments of a university. In the real world, the lines can be somewhat blurred and therefore adaptability is a great trait to have and that sometimes comes from crossing over into new disciplines.

There are also the possibilities of doing multiple internships in a college career. I recently met a woman who calls herself the "internship queen". While at the University of Central Florida, Lauren Berger completed 15 internships in four years. Lauren runs a web site on the topic of internships (internqueen.com) and travels the country speaking to students about internships. Perhaps you won't reach the prolific internship levels of Ms. Berger but you could do 2 or 3 internships before you graduate – especially if you begin planning early and making valuable contacts.

Year –by-Year Plan

The best way to plan for a great internship is to start in your freshman year and complete a series of activities that will have you well positioned (by your junior year) to land and complete a great internship.

In your freshman year:

1. Become familiar with the requirements, policies and procedures of your college's internship program.

2. Discover the types of clubs, campus activities, and service learning opportunities that relate to your major and participate. These activities and memberships can provide excellent leads for future internships. Through involvement in campus organizations and volunteerism, you can develop your leadership and communication skills and learn about working as a team, planning projects, delegating, promoting special events and meeting deadlines – all important skills to take into an internship. Student Activities and the Office of Civic Engagement are two great resources to help you identify opportunities.

3. Create your first draft of your résumé. This document should be updated at least once a year while in college. Make it a habit to edit and revise your résumé at the conclusion of each academic year and each time before you submit it to an employer as a result of a job or internship posting.

4. Find a good summer job and ideally, one that might offer you a higher-level position as an intern in later years.

In your sophomore year:

1. Make an appointment with an advisor or an internship director to discuss the possibility of doing a summer internship (after the completion of your sophomore year).

2. Learn how to use the tools and search engines available through your career planning center that may help you learn about internship opportunities. Learning to use these tools can help you when you are ready to devise your internship search plan. Some colleges offer internship workshops or orientation sessions to help students begin their planning and search for a great internship. Inquire through your advisor or the Career Resource Center of your school.

3. If you are interested in semester long/full-time internships, explore internships away from school via providers such as The Washington Center and other organizations that will partner with your school.

4. Attend career fairs, network with professionals in fields that interest you, and explore opportunities in your hometown. Some colleges will host internship roundtables: a special "speed networking" version of a career fair typically consists of a combination of "networking" visits with employers and small group discussions.

5. Very early (January) in the spring semester, update your résumé and write a cover letter that can be used as a template to prepare internship inquiry or application letters. Apply early -- application deadlines that are one semester prior to internship start dates are common. This is particularly true for popular, well-known, national internships. Learn the deadlines.

6. In the late spring or early summer, prepare a list of organizations that you would like to intern for and prepare an associated list of contacts. To do this use career resource planning tools, web sites such as Indeed.com, Monster.com, blogs, etc. and draw upon contacts you have made via campus clubs and activities.

In your junior and senior years:

1. Participate in at least one internship in either your fall or spring semester or do a summer internship after your spring semester, junior year.

2. Use the contacts you have made in your internship(s) to compile a list of employers to which you will apply for a full-time position upon graduation.

Gaining Credit

Early in the game, students should understand how to gain credit for an internship. I speak to high school seniors who are looking at our school at an event we call *Discovery Days*. It is a type of open house – tours and Q&A sessions for both prospective students and their parents. I tell the students to think about doing an internship in their junior year of college and how we can help them get credit for such an experience. I want the general process of earning internship credit to be in the minds of our students and even prospective students – as early as possible. It is never too early to plan for your internships.

You need to understand how internships work at your school. Get your hands on the materials your college distributes to explain the policies and procedures of the internship program. Perhaps there are handouts, a brochure, or a web site that can give you a first pass at understanding how your school's internship program works. Are the credits awarded under the supervision of a professor? Is there a required internship class that is coupled with the experience? What must you do to get your internship approved? Does the school match you with an internship provider or are you on your own?

Many schools require that the student find the internship and compete for the position – just like trying to land a job. There are a few reasons for this but the primary reason is usually that there aren't enough internships to go around. Therefore, instead of running a placement service, most schools run a clearing service – acting as an "agent" – posting and promoting open positions for interns but never actually placing a student in a slot or matching a student's résumé to internship posting requirements.

At the Charlton College of Business, my office acts as a facilitator in that we help promote internship positions that are open, help students get their résumé in order, and provide information but we don't play matchmaker. It is up to the student to put their best foot forward, interview well, present a well-written cover letter and résumé, and land the position. Once a student gets the offer from the internship provider, they come to me to gain approval to enroll in our internship class.

To gain internship credits, our school requires students to take a semester-long internship class. The class runs concurrent with the internship. We require that students follow these steps:

1. Land an "approved" internship.

2. Meet some simple criteria (minimum GPA, junior standing, and business major).

3. Enroll and complete our internship class.

4. Meet the minimum number of hours in the field (135 hours).

Our internship class, which began as a 1 hour per week traditional, face-to-face class is now 100% online. It requires weekly assignments, work journals, and online discussions. It also requires a term paper that documents the experience and achievement of internship goals.

At other schools, internship credit is awarded by a sponsoring faculty member who oversees the experience and often requires assignments such as a term paper and written evaluation by a supervisor from the internship provider. That type of arrangement is sometimes called experiential learning.

The key for the student is to learn exactly how the school handles internships so they can also understand exactly what will be expected and the steps needed to gain credit.

Some colleges place students into internships. Those schools commit resources to not only recruit good internship providers both in business and the nonprofit sector, but also offer matchmaking services – screen internship applicants and matching the student to the internship position. That is not the case at my school. Our internships are the result of a competitive process. Students apply directly to the employer, attempt to gain interviews, and do their best to get a job offer. With that model, it is imperative that students understand how to write a good cover letter and résumé, how to dress, and of course, how to come across professionally and prepared in an interview.

Some schools only allow students to participate in "approved" internships while others allow students to work with employers to develop internships. We actively promote "approved internship" postings to our students but we also allow students to propose an internship. For example, at the University of Massachusetts Dartmouth, I approve internships after reviewing data submitted by employers. I post these opportunities to a blog and encourage our students to apply.

Frequently, students submit brief proposals detailing an internship arrangement with a new employer. In those cases, I review the information, call the employer and discuss the situation, and sometimes make a site visit before I will approve the internship. Some of our highest quality internships have been derived by a student driven process.

If a student's school allows them to land their own internship, they should start early to think about a plan of action. Students will want to come up with a list of potential internship providers and then write cover letters, résumés, and emails to "leads" in the area.

Cover letters or emails should state interest in an internship, disclose that you are seeking credit, and provide background information on your college's internship program.

I suggest that our students include our internship brochure and also point potential intern employers to our internship web site (www.umassd.edu/charlton/internship.cfm). There they can read the policies and procedures that I follow to run the program, learn the steps to take to get an internship approved and to apply to earn credit, and learn about other resources like blogs, tweet, and job portals that we utilize.

In some cases, I suggest that students give potential employers a document that I wrote entitled: *Designing a Successful Internship*, so that the employer understands the commitment and what it will take to make it a winning experience.

Learn the Deadlines

Know the deadlines for applying for internships. Some large companies require submissions many months ahead of time, for internship applications. Here's a sampling of deadlines for summer internships:

- White House – deadline for application is February 26th
- NBA – deadline for application is December 15th
- National Public Radio – deadline for application is February 15th
- Reebok – deadline for application is March 15.
- The Washington Center – competitive deadline for spring semesters in D.C. late September.

As you can see, the deadlines vary from one organization to another. Students interested in summer internships may need to apply as early as mid-December and in some cases can apply as late as mid-March. Many of the smaller companies have deadlines that are much closer in time to the start of the associated semester. For example, although some larger internship programs require students to apply for a fall internship before late May, it isn't uncommon for employers to accept résumés right up till the start of the fall semester.

Two of our largest intern providers, have often continued to accept applications right up till the first week of school (dependent upon their hiring plans). The same is true in the summer. I have some internship providers who require students send in résumés for summer internships early in the spring and then there are many others who notify me of postings as late as June and early July.

The Application Process

When you apply for an internship, you usually need to write a cover letter and résumé – just as if you were applying for a job. Read the internship posting carefully as sometimes the letter can be submitted as an email with the résumé as an attachment. Many internship sponsors, such as Reebok, Staples, many of the large accounting firms, require that you apply via their human resources portal. Be sure to follow all the requirements of the portal and attach all necessary documents.

Read all internship listings very carefully to see what documents are needed to apply. If transcripts and reference letters are required, be sure to allow ample time to get these documents together. Often digital versions of a transcript are required and you should be able to either scan a hardcopy or request a PDF version from your school's registrar. On a few occasions I have helped harried students put together an application for a competitive internship by scanning documents at the 11th hour. You don't want to be like that. Plan early and get all your ducks in order.

Be ready to send an error free, grammatically correct résumé and cover letter to the employer. Have someone who is a good writer check over your documents. Your first impression will be set by those documents. At the Charlton College of Business, I recommend that my students bring their cover letters and résumés to our career development center where someone proofreads them and gives advice on how to present a well-written cover letter and résumé. This process will also serve you well when you start applying for full-time, permanent positions in your senior year and also if you need to prepare an application package for an MBA program.

Rarely will internship providers request references but if you run into that requirement, provide all references with a copy of your résumé.

Checklist: Professional Work Environment

- ✓ Start early to think about and research internship possibilities in your area of interest and preferred regions of the country
- ✓ Make an effort to meet professionals in your chosen field who could be good contacts in the future (develop your network)
- ✓ Devise a calendar of events and actions that will guide your career development throughout your college years. People in the career development center of your college can help
- ✓ Understand your schools process for approving an internship and granting credit for internship experiences. If there is a class, understand its requirements
- ✓ Know the deadlines for application to an employer and approval of internships by your school

Chapter 3

Finding a Good Internship

INTERNSHIP PROGRAMS AT COLLEGES are run by deans, department chairs, internship directors and other administrators. When students at my business school want an internship they get in touch with me or they search online sources for open opportunities.

Researching and identifying an internship usually requires more time and preparation than most students realize. You must remain patient and positive; great leads may come at any time and from a variety of sources.

Be creative and take advantage of any opportunities that give you the chance to communicate with an employer. I encourage students to search on their own; to explore what is out there and to come back to me with proposals. One thing that all business students should know is that many employers are looking for interns and many others could be easily convinced that an internship is a good idea for their organization.

Area employers contact our college with internship opportunities almost weekly. In turn, these opportunities are promoted to business students via email, web site postings, Twitter, Facebook, blogs and word of mouth. Faculty make announcements in class and our student advisors point students in the right direction. So by a variety of communications, interested students are informed about the various internship opportunities. Ultimately, it is the student's responsibility to be tapped into those communications and to respond to postings in a timely manner with a well-done résumé and cover letter (or email message.)

Sometimes we (the college of business) have almost nothing to do with students landing internships. Many business students discover excellent internship opportunities on their own and submit them for approval. Many times these are the best situations in part because the student digs to uncover them and then develops a real sense of ownership with the internship. But I remind you, I think a diversified approach to finding good internships is the way to go so look at all possible sources of internship leads.

I have had students work with our Career Resource Center to find a good opportunity or send résumés to area companies that they find interesting. I have had students uncover great summer internship opportunities by leaving their résumés and our internship brochure with businesses and nonprofits back in their hometowns and often, students will get a call back for an interview.

One student in particular landed an excellent accounting internship with a regional CPA firm that was about 30 miles from our campus. The company is Kahn, Litwin, Renza & Co. (KLR): a certified public accountants and business consultants. KLR is one of the largest regional CPA firms in southern New England. Our student was the first student from our school to successfully complete an internship with the firm and by Thanksgiving of her senior year, was assured a well paying full-time job with that firm. The good folks at Kahn, Litwin, Renza & Co. have continued to recruit our students and from that one very positive internship experience, other opportunities have spawned. That's a success story that I always recall when students ask me how to uncover good opportunities.

Some schools, like the world famous Fuqua School of business at Duke University, solicit the assistance of students who have already gone through the process of landing an internship. Each year the career management center at Duke selects sixty or so students that are career fellows—second-year students that have already been through the job-search process and have had successful summer internships. They work with the first-year students, by industry and functional area, on résumés, cover letters, and mock interviews. The career fellow approach is an outstanding idea.

Other business schools rely very heavily on their alumni to bring students aboard as interns. At the Charlton College of Business we have a great relationship with alumni working at a local CPA firm, Fernandes and Charest P.C., of Westport, Massachusetts takes on a couple of our interns every year and the firm has more than a handful of UMASS Dartmouth alumni as full-time employees. The same is true with Textron headquartered in Providence, RI. Their controller group has several of our alums who come back to us each semester to recruit Charlton College of Business (accounting and finance majors) for their government reporting function. An alumni network of established professionals that can advocate for interns inside the firm is a powerful internship supply chain.

Research and Hustle

If you are interested in landing a great internship you will need to do some research and you will need to hustle. Internships are competitive situations. The opportunity probably won't be handed to you. Professors, deans, internship directors, and others at your school can sometimes advocate for you or recommend you to an employer for an internship position. However, don't count on that. You need to be proactive, prepared, and eager.

If your school has an internship director, meet with him or her to find out how internship announcements are made. Are they blasted out via email, posted on a blog, posted on Facebook, entered into a software system, or set up on the web? Does the school have an internship Twitter? My Twitter for internships is @bizinternships. I tell students who are in the hunt for an internship that responding quickly to my Tweets might be key. Many times, especially for internships in small companies and nonprofits, the odds of landing an internship increase dramatically for those who respond quickly.

If your college has a Career Resource Center, visit the center and find out how they can help you land a good internship. There are people at your school that have a passion for internships. Identify who they are and begin to work with them to uncover great opportunities, but keep in mind that the most you can hope for is guidance. You will need to do most of the work.

Think about the type of internship that will help you meet your personal goals. Think about your reasons for wanting an internship. Make a list of your interests, skills, career aspirations, and what exactly you want to accomplish in the 15 weeks or so that you will be interning. For example, an accounting student planning on a career in public accounting might look at internship with a local CPA firm or a summer internship with one of the national accounting firms. However, if an accounting major wants to go into management accounting, an internship as a staff accountant or internal auditor might make more sense.

Ask yourself some more questions:

- What do I want to get out of an internship?

- Do I want to work during the summer or the fall or spring semesters?

- Can I afford an unpaid internship?

It may be that your search for an internship will have constraints. You need to define those constraints. There may be a particular semester that makes the most sense or it might be that you need to be paid to keep afloat. Constraints are part of life. Identify your constraining factors and focus your search appropriately. If you give yourself enough time, utilize the right resources and work hard enough, you will find an opportunity that will match up well with what you want to accomplish. Do your research, reflect on what you want and your constraints, and hustle.

I can't emphasize enough the need to be proactive in your search. Don't wait for someone to find you an internship. One of the valuable aspects of an internship is that you get to call some of the shots. You have a chance to be proactive and shape your learning experience right from the start.

Explore possibilities on your own. I tell students to review job listings in the Sunday classified ads of our local papers: the Boston Globe, Providence Journal, New Bedford Standard Times, and the Fall River Herald News. Those are the papers of the major cities in our region that list job openings. Although companies rarely advertise internships in the newspaper, you may discover a contact person to whom you can send your own cover letter and résumé inquiring or proposing an internship.

Developing "leads" is a key to landing your own internship. Consider sending a letter of inquiry and your résumé to prospective employers. An example inquiry letter is contained towards the end of this chapter. Tailor that example to your own search.

Search online job banks for internships. Perhaps your Career Resource Center can help you learn how to do this in the most effective and efficient manner. A service such as MonsterTrak.com is a useful portal for students looking for the first job or an internship. Indeed.com is another one that I like to use as it lets me set up email alerts - messages letting me know that internship postings have hit the net based on criteria that I set (i.e., accounting internships in Boston, MA.) Since online services are updated each day, you need to visit frequently and respond quickly to any internship opportunities that interest you. I tell students to visit my internship blog everyday to see if there is anything new (www.businessinternships.blogspot.com/). Habits like that will pay off. A consistent, relentless strategy of checking resources is an example of the necessary persistence and hustle that separate those students who find good opportunities and those who do not. I sincerely think that persistence and hustle in the internship search (and the job search) is more valuable than smarts.

Checking web resources is not enough. You should also get out there and talk to people. What are some of your options? Attend a career fair (on campus or off campus) and discuss your desire to land a great internship with recruiters. Some employers will only be interested in students who can work full-time or who are on the verge of graduating. However, some employers will recognize talent when they see it and be open to developing an internship. Keep in mind that companies that participate in job fairs are trying to recruit talent and an internship is definitely a recruiting tool, and a low risk one at that. Follow-up any potential leads that you cultivate at a job fair with a résumé and cover letter. Follow-up those correspondences with an email and a phone call.

Let your business professors, your parents, and your parents' colleagues, friends, and neighbors know that you are looking for an internship. They know people in the industry who may be looking for an intern. You might consider a job shadow engagement or an informational interview of one of your parent's friends or a relative who are established in the business. One of my brothers is a successful venture capitalist and he is happy to sit down with students who are interested in his field and give them advice. Other professionals will allow you to follow them around for a work day (job shadow) so you can see what a typical day is like in their profession. Job shadowing is like a mini-internship without any heavy lifting. Some colleges offer externships - short-term internships-like projects that carry no credit but offer experience.

Tap into your professors. They may seem ensconced in their ivory towers but many are much more than that. Many professors are involved in their communities, active in the chamber of commerce and other community groups, have relatives and friends that are established in their careers and can provide internship leads. Accounting professors know practitioners, operations management faculty know people who run factories, and marketing professors know people who run advertising agencies. These are valuable contacts and part of a faculty member's job should be to connect students with the business community. I think of myself as a facilitator of contacts or a type of conduit through which my students get to meet business managers and leaders. That is one of the most valuable aspects of my position.

Talk to other students who have completed internships. Your peers are a great source of information regarding internships. They can give you firsthand knowledge about the employer and whether they think the experience was worth the time and effort. Networking through fellow students and friends can be the best way to land a great internship. This is a powerful internship network at our college. Students who complete successful internships tell their friends. I receive countless emails and phone calls from students who tell me their friend completed an internship at XYZ Corporation and recommended the experience.

Have business cards made that you can hand out to people that you meet. Companies like VistaPrint (www.vistaprint.com) and Staples - the office supply company periodically offer free business cards.[3] VistaPrint typically gives away 250 copies of a basic business card as a way of introducing customers to its online services.[4] Take advantage of that offer.

Subscribe to an email alert service that can tell you when an internship posting has been made on the web. I subscribe to one through a web site called Indeed.com and it has been quite fruitful. They send me an email once a day based on the keywords. For example, I receive an email alert for any web job posting that included the words: "Internships in Massachusetts." As a result, I have been able to alert our business students to internship openings with companies such as State Street Bank, Proctor and Gamble, the New England Patriots (Kraft Sports Group), the Boston Bruins, State Street Coporation, Fidelity Investments, Nike, Reebok, and PricewaterhouseCoopers, just to name a few.

If you are interested in finding your own internship, one strategy you can try is to send a letter of inquiry and your résumé to companies and organizations in the region. Many career planning experts discourage this practice as they say the success rate with this "old fashion" method is low and there are better ways to spend your time. That generalization is probably true. However, I know many students who have used a focused approach to the old "blast out résumés" approach and have had success. An example is the accounting student who I referred to previously in this chapter who landed an internship with the Providence, RI based KLR (CPA firm). She send out résumés to a list of regional CPA firms and got an interview with one of the best.

---

[3] Staples, a Massachusetts based corporation has a rich history of providing quality internships. If you are from the Boston area or can come to Massachusetts for a summer internship, check out the internship opportunities on Staples web site.

[4] VistaPrint is a large technology company based in Massachusetts. The Boston Globe recently listed VistaPrint as number 27 on its list of the Top 100 companies in Massachusetts. VistaPrint has more than 2,700 employees and is headquarter in Lexington, Massachusetts. Its market value is greater than $2 billion (as of July 2011). Maybe they would like to hire a few iterns?

Obviously, in conducting a mail campaign, finding a mailing list of companies is the key. You can use the yellow pages but you must find a way to focus the yellow page search. Be careful to identify organizations that are likely to offer internships and are of interest to you. Some business oriented newspapers offer a book of lists. For example, in our region there is a newspaper called the Providence Business News (PBN). Providence, RI is the largest metropolitan area within a 30 mile radius of our University.

Annually, PBN publishes its Book of Lists. These lists include the largest organizations in the region in such categories as Accounting Firms, Advertising Agencies, Banks, Hospitals, Manufacturers, and Insurance companies. By perusing that publication, students my come upon a company that is of interest to them or perhaps they may have friends or family members who work for one of the companies and may be able to connect them an internship sponsor.

I have also suggested that students look at lists of the largest employers within a fifty mile radius of our campus. That type of information can be found on the web or perhaps obtained from local chambers of commerce and in some cases, from the Career Resource Center of your school. Our internship program is operated out of our college of business but in some schools, the Career Resource Center takes a more active role in identifying possible internship providers. In addition, many colleges and universities are successful in connecting alumni with current students for internship match-making. Your school's alumni office or career center might have ideas on how you can make such a connection.

Cover Letter

Below is a form letter that I give to our students to use in a search for an internship. I encourage them to customize this template to meet their specific needs.

Your Name
Street Address
City, State Zip
Phone Number
Email Address

Date

Company Name
Name and Title of Person
Street Address
City, State Zip

Dear _____:

I am a (junior or senior) (accounting, finance, marketing, MIS, management) major at the Charlton College of Business, University of Massachusetts Dartmouth. My program allows me to earn three business elective credits by interning at a local company or agency. I am interested in developing an internship with your organization and have included my résumé for your review.

Internships-for-credit require a minimum of 9 hours per week for a total of 135 hours on the job along with the completion of an internship course. My internship will be monitored by a business professor and I will be required to complete several assignments, including a term paper, as part of my internship course.

You can learn more about the Charlton College of Business internship program by visiting:

www.umassd.edu/charlton/internship.cfm

I would also be happy to meet with you or another representative of your company to explore this possibility. I can be reached at (telephone number) or by email at (email address).

Sincerely,

Your name

Make a Proposal

Once you have found an internship, depending on the policies and procedures of your school, you may need to present the internship to a sponsoring professor or your internship director for approval. Some schools require that you prepare an internship proposal that describes the job or project that you will be working on. The proposal must contain enough information for your professor or internship director to make a decision as to the creditworthiness of the opportunity. Be sure to include within your proposal all of the following (and please check to see if other information is required by your school):

- Description of the company including the mission, location, sales and market coverage. Please include your web URL (if you have it).
- Overview of the internship objectives
- Primary duties and responsibilities
- What you will learn from this experience
- Job title
- Compensation
- Skills required
- Hours of work
- Start and end dates
- Name of primary supervisor
- How will the student(s) be evaluated?
- Additional company contacts (if applicable)
- Name and title of the person providing this information (information should be gathered in collaboration with someone from the internship providing organization)

Internships in Faraway Places

Summer internships offer a chance to travel and earn internship credit. Our program offers distant learning through our myCourses (online management learning) system. We have had interns working in England, Ireland, France, and Germany while earning credit through the University of Massachusetts Dartmouth. We have had several students work as interns in Washington DC (through the Washington Center) and in Florida for Disney. In the summer of 2009 and 2010 we had interns working in Cooperstown, New York. A friend of mine runs a software development company in India called Extentia Information Technology and he has a vibrant and successful internship program called Connect

Global Internship (www.extentia.com). Extentia prides itself in allowing student interns to become immersed for a semester in the development of software solutions.

Some international companies will sponsor an intern from the states. For example, Extentia Information Technology recruits U.S. college students to spend a semester interning at their headquarters in Pune. They provide living quarters and a small stipend to help cover other living expenses.

When students approach me about international internships, I ask them to gather as much information as possible and to discuss their plans with our Study Abroad office as these arrangements can be complex and our Study Abroad office understands the complexities much better than I do. International internships are a wonderful way to get real world experience with a global flavor. If you are a student who is interested in an international internship, meet with all the parties at your college who can make that happen including the internship director, director of study aboard programs and your international studies office. It might be possible to intern abroad and also earn credit from exchange courses you take in a foreign country.

Checklist: Finding a good internship

✓ Search for internships using college resources such as Career Development Centers and online databases of internship postings such as Experience.com and Internships.com.

✓ Search for internships on such services as Indeed.com and set up email alerts so you can be notified when internships matching your keyword searches hit the web.

✓ Prepare a résumé and cover letter and drop them off at the human resources department at local businesses that interest you. Follow up in a few days with a phone call.

✓ Let your business professors, your parents, and your parents' colleagues, friends, and neighbors know that you are looking for an internship. They know people in the industry who may be looking for an intern.

✓ Talk to other students who have completed internships. Your peers are a great source of information regarding internships.

✓ Attend college-sponsored events that attract alumni and be ready to introduce yourself and inquire about internship opportunities.

Chapter 4

Top 10 Ways to Find an Internship

ALTHOUGH THE LAST TWO CHAPTERS give advice on how to land a good internship, I though a third chapter on the subject couldn't hurt because without a clear strategy of finding an internship, the discussion of internships is really moot. Being a fan of David Letterman and his nightly *Top Ten Lists*, I have prepared my own top ten list – the Top 10 Ways to Find an Internship. I did this because so many students are lost when it comes to developing an approach to uncover internship opportunities and so a short and focused list might be a good way to start.

I tell students that, just as is the case in finding a full-time job upon graduation, they may need several approaches to landing an internship.

10. **Blasting out résumés** – if you know of a company or a nonprofit that you would like to intern at, send them your résumé. But caution - mass blasting of résumés is very inefficient. It is best if you know someone at the company or at least get a referral from a friend, relative, or neighbor. Create a contact/mailing list using names of people at the company but if you don't have a name and still want to take a chance, send a letter and résumé (or an email and résumé attachment) to the human resources department. If the targeted firm utilizes interns, the HR people will know and they can get your résumé to the right person.

You might think about scanning job sites if your college has their own job portal. I also point students to lists of top employers in various categories. For example, you can find a list on the Internet or in our region there is a publication called the *Providence Business News*, which lists the top ten companies in various categories such as the top 10 CPA firms in Rhode Island. I know a student who sent résumés to the top five CPA firm, landed an internship and then eventually got an excellent job offer.

9. Vault.com , Hotjobs, InternshipKing and other web portals – You must harness the Net to your advantage – especially if you are looking for internships from outside the 50 mile radius of campus – as is often the case for students looking to work back at home during the summer break.

Fortune magazine recently called Vault.com "The best place on the Web to prepare for a job search." The site has some good resources that might offer you some strategies and videos on top rated internships.

Hotjobs.yahoo.com is another place to search for internships. Use the keyword: Internship and search for a specific state: (i.e., MA).

A relatively new portal, InternshipKing.com was founded by Ted Williams (not the Red Sox great but a person with a passion for internships). One nice feature of InternshipKing.com is that it allows students to provide feedback on their experiences with national firms that utilize interns. It also provides succinct profiles of these firms and their internship programs.

8. Indeed.com – Indeed is another Internet resource/search engine that I have had luck with. I list it as a separate *Top 10 List* item because I know of students who have used Indeed to their advantage and Indeed.com has "fed" me with a number of interesting opportunities. I was able to refer a student to a Boston Bruins marketing internship (National Hockey League) that she successfully landed. Indeed.com has also been the source of information on internship postings for many other internships our students have landed such as a fine human resources management internship with Lowes Home Improvement and an operations management internship with Bose, maker of high quality stereo speakers and headphones.

With Indeed.com, you can conduct keyword searches such as: "Marketing Internship, Boston, MA" and get listings of all postings with those keywords that have recently hit the Internet. And here's the best part: you can specify to have Indeed.com send you email alerts when job postings with your keywords hit the net. I receive emails from Indeed.com almost every day notifying me of internships in Springfield, Worcester, Boston, Massachusetts, Rhode Island, etc. Sometimes some very interesting opportunities are discovered.

7. Experience.com – Experience.com is a job and career planning portal that is run by a Boston-based firm called Experience Inc., founded by Jennifer Floren, a smart, dynamic entrepreneur. Ms. Floren founded the company in response to what she felt was a need to provide better career information to college students. The Career Planning portal of Experience.com is called eRecruiting and it is the standard used by many colleges and universities throughout the U.S. Check to see if your university uses eRecruiting and find out how you can log on and search for internships.

6. **The Washington Center (TWC)** – If you are looking for an internship in business or government and want to have your experience in the Washington DC. area, they this should be number one on your top ten list. I have had several students' complete Washington Center internships and I have visited internship sites in the DC area and am nothing but impressed with the program.

Our university has a great relationship with the Washington Center, the premier provider of internships in Washington DC. Twice each year, the Washington Center representative visits our campus to discuss their excellent programs. TWC helps you find internships in government, nonprofits, and the profit sectors in DC. If you are interested in TWC, visit their web site: www.twc.edu and then see if your campus has a representative – a liaison who can help you learn more about how this excellent program works.

5. **A faculty member** – Let your favorite faculty member know that you're looking for an internship. Go see the professor during office hours or mention it after class. Sometimes timing and luck is better than being smart. There is some truth to the idea that you might be in the right place at the right time with internships. Sometimes a faculty member will have just heard about a project, job, or internship that might be a great match. I can't tell you how many times this has happened.

One recent incident has become almost legendary at our college. A student told me that he wanted to intern for Narragansett Brewing, a local beer company. That evening, the CEO of Narragansett was giving a lecture at our technology center. I suggested to the student that he attend the lecture, ask some questions and introduce himself to the CEO. The student followed my advice and the CEO was so impressed he gave him an internship. Sometimes luck is better than smarts but I think this student has both going for him!

4. **Friends and Family, Alumni, etc**. – Use all your contacts to find an internship. Who do Mom, Dad, Uncle Charlie, Auntie Edna, the CPA next door, etc. work for and can they help get you into an internship? Learn how to network. That's where some great opportunities will be born. Our accounting majors are real good at using networks to find internships. They start with their families and make contacts through their involvement in the Accounting Association – a club on campus. If you join a club and hear a speaker who is interesting, ask the speaker about internships, get their business card etc. There are so many opportunities to get the word out that you are looking for an internship. You need an

army of contacts on your side. Alumni also like to help. If you know an alumnus who works in an area or a company that interests you, talk to them about internships.

Our students have been using Facebook to discuss internships and I have hundreds of friends on my Facebook, most of them are students looking for internships. Facebook might help you make connections but also use the old fashion way of making contacts; meet people and tell them about your goals.

3. **Referrals from peers who have completed internships** – Listen to your peers. If a student has had a good internship, ask them for a contact person or if they know if another position is open. Word-of-mouth is one of the best ways to land an internship and the best part is that you can probably trust your peer's perception of whether it was a good experience.

2. **Local nonprofits** – Don't ignore local nonprofits. Many are eager to get some good interns on board. In our area, the Southcoast Hospital Group is the largest employer in the region and they have shown great interest in getting our students in as interns. We also have relied on The New Bedford Whaling Museum (www.whalingmuseum.org), Zeiterion Performing Arts Center (www.zeiterion.org), CEDC (VITA Program), the Fall River and New Bedford Chambers of Commerce as they have all utilized interns in the past. Nonprofits usually don't pay interns (although a small percentage of nonprofits do pay interns, usually at minimum wage rates). Especially during tough economic times when companies tend to shy away from paid internships, a nonprofit might be your best bet for an excellent internship experience.

1. **The Internship Blog and emails** – This is a special number one reason – and possibly only pertinent to my home university (but your college may have one so I recommend you ask your internship coordinator.) I receive internship announcements from local companies and I usually send targeted emails to juniors and seniors letting them know what's available. For example, if I know of a CPA firm internship, accounting juniors and seniors get the email. Marketing internships get sent to marketing majors and so on. Just about all emails also get posted on my Internship Blog:

www.businessinternships.blogspot.com

I tell our students to make it a habit to check the blog for current listings but all check out the archives of the blog for all postings and if there is anything there that seems of interest, don't hesitate to send a quick email to the contact person to see if an internship might be available and if not, when one might come open.

Check with the Career Resource Center of your college or with the internship director of your school and ask if they post opportunities to a blog or send out a periodic email alert. If you see anything of interest posted in those electronic media, respond quickly. Internships are often competitive situations – just like trying to land a full-time job. So act fast!

Checklist: Top 10 ways to land an internship

- ✓ 10. Blasting out résumés
- ✓ 9. Vault, Yahoo, and other portals
- ✓ 8. Indeed.com email alerts
- ✓ 7. Experience.com
- ✓ 6. The Washington Center
- ✓ 5. Professors
- ✓ 4. Friends, Family and Alumni
- ✓ 3. Fellow students who have completed internships
- ✓ 2. Local nonprofits
- ✓ 1. Blogs (mine is www.businessinternships.blogspot.com)

Chapter 5

Making the Most of an Internship

THE GREATEST ACHIEVEMENT with our internship program, other than seeing a young person do well and land a great full-time job, is having an employer call and ask for more interns. It is then that I know that students have made the most of their internship and have helped create a strong relationship between our school and an outside organization (a company or nonprofit organization). I tell our students that there are long-term implications to almost every internship. If a student leaves a legacy of good work, excellent behavior, and a winning attitude, more opportunities from that same provider will accrue to future students of the Charlton College of Business. In that way, every student is an ambassador of our college.

Your internship should not be taken lightly. If you are interested in an internship because you think it might be an easy way to pick up some credits, you are in it for the wrong reason. College internships should not be extended field trips or an easy way to earn a grade. They are opportunities for you to learn a great deal and to show an employer what you can do. They are not so much an opportunity to pad your résumé or boost your GPA as they are a chance to get some experience, make connections, and learn from an experienced mentor.

An internship is quite different from a class. In an internship, you will use a different set of skills and knowledge than what is needed in the classroom. The focus is more on what you do (rather than on what you know.) Despite the fact that most internship providers are giving something back and are typically very open to helping students learn, most are also looking for some value in return. There is the win/win of internships. Internship providers, whether they are profit seeking entities, nonprofits, or government agencies, are looking for you to be a contributor, to add some value to the organization. They are looking for students who are eager to do anything to help and do it with enthusiasm, confidence, and grace. They are looking for some freshness and energy and you should be ready to provide that in a very professional manner.

Test and Then Learn

Companies want interns who understand that the real world is very different from the classroom. The real world often tests first, and then provides the lesson. In your internship, you will find yourself doing things, performing tasks, and completing assignments and then learning the lesson; just the opposite of academia where we give the lesson and then the test. You won't have a set of instructions, a user manual, cookbooks with recipes or text books full of exercises to guide you. You must find a way to get the job done, to meet a real world test.

You have learned many lessons in your years of school and you are a reservoir of a great deal of information. In an internship, usefulness of information depends on what you do with what you know. It is how you relate your knowledge to the situation at hand. The challenge is how to apply your knowledge, skills, and abilities in practical ways - in ways that solve problems.

In your internship, you will find that people-skills are more important in the field than in the classroom. Teamwork, persuasion, communication, and relating well to others will all be important skills. This is a conclusion that my student interns arrive at almost 100% of the time.

Closing the Gap

Students who have never held a professional job often have a great deal of anxiety about the gap between what they know and what is expected of them in the real world. Some have even gone as far as to tell me that they think they need to avoid the real world and head into an MBA program because they don't believe they have what it takes to get the job done in the real world. I feel bad when I hear that a student doesn't believe they are ready for the work world. It seems like we have all failed when that happens. Internships can help close "work-world readiness gap." I can't tell you how many students have commented in their final papers that they gained significant real world experience, proved some things to themselves, and gained the valuable confidence that comes with getting done the daily work of an organization.

Your internship will help you cope with the anxiety of applying your knowledge and skills to new situations. Don't be frustrated by the "lack of fit" between what is learned in class versus what is done in the field. There certainly is a gap between book learning and case studies and the real challenges of the business world. As hard as we may try to introduce reality based learning through projects, simulations, and case studies, professors can never provide an environment in the classroom that rivals the demands and realities of the real world. Again, the internship can help you see the problems and solutions of the real world.

If you stay positive throughout your internship, have confidence and work in a persistence manner, you will apply what you have learned in ways you never dreamed you could.

Strive to Add Value with the Top Priority of Learning

Although you should strive to make the internship experience a win-win situation (a win for both you and the employer/provider), keep in mind that you are primarily in an internship to learn. Being a strong contributor will take time and is a worthy goal but start out by trying to learn as much as you can.

Take advantage of every learning opportunity. Take tours, field trips, attend meetings and seminars. One of our interns worked at Nestle Waters in Raynham, Massachusetts. Nestle Waters owns several recognizable bottled water brands such as Poland Springs, Deer Park, Ice Mountain, and Perrier. The Raynham, Massachusetts facility is a call center. Our intern's responsibilities involved mostly trouble shooting customer problems – an important customer service function but one that requires almost constant engagement on the phone.

To enhance the learning experience of the Nestle Waters internship, the student was allowed to take field trips to the wells where the spring water is derived, rode with the delivery personnel on daily truck routes, and attended in-house management seminars. These extra activities combined with the daily responsibilities of the internship provided the student with a comprehensive view of the Nestle Waters value chain. There is no doubt that this experience was an excellent learning experience. If your internship is very focused and you want learn more, mention to your mentor/supervisor that you'd like to see and experience more. Most internship mentors will go out of their way to accommodate you.

What's Your Question?

Asking questions, lots of questions, is always the best way to learn new things. If you see or hear something during the course of your internship that you don't understand, get clarification by asking questions. Curiosity is the way to learn. So many of the reference letters I write for students for jobs and graduate school mention curiosity. Employers love to see curious students. Curiosity may have "killed the cat" (an old saying) but it will make you smarter in school, in an internship and in your career.

Ask questions and never fake your knowledge. If you are open about how much you need to learn, your internship will be much more beneficial than if you feign your knowledge. Interns are not expected to know everything and therefore you can use your ignorance and vulnerability to your advantage.

When starting an internship be ready to learn but also be open about how much you want to learn. Some of our students sign up for out VITA program in the spring semester. As previously discussed in this book, VITA stands for Volunteer Income Tax Assistance – a federal program that helps low-income people get tax return preparation assistance. Many of our VITA students enter the program with one goal in mind - they want to learn how to do tax returns. However, many of them soon learn that if they keep their eyes open wide, they will learn about how to interview, collect data, communicate with people and learn how a nonprofit works to serve the needs of disadvantaged folks.

If you are taking an internship class in conjunction with your internship, bring questions to class for discussion. Use the internship professor as a resource. Believe me, internship professors love to hear questions from the field and it is great to have other students hear your questions and perhaps offer their take on the situation. In our internship class, I monitor online discussions between students. Often to get the ball rolling, I pose questions or ask for comments but once the ball is rolling my students become active participants in very thoughtful discussions that add to the learning experience of the internship.

Knowing What is Expected

Be clear about what is expected of you. Ask for a job description from your supervisor and agree on internship goals and objectives with your supervisor. In our internship class, one of the first assignments is for students to set goals and to write their own job description. I believe that goals and a specific and detailed job description is a good starting point. I am sure that if you are earning credit at your college or university for your internship, you will be required to develop clear goals and objectives for the internship.

Also along the lines of knowing what is expected of you, you should be sure to follow company rules as to dress, conduct, punctuality, adherence to policies, etc. If your internship involves dealing with the public, clients, or customers, be sure to understand company policies and procedures. Most well run organizations have written policies and procedures and will let you read them. You can learn a great deal from reading policy and procedure manuals.[5]

For example, most companies require employees to answer the phone in a particular way. Be sure to understand what is expected of you. One of our student interns was manning the phone system of a CPA firm while the receptionist was at lunch one day. She was shocked to find out that one of the partners of the firm had called in and was disappointed at the way she answered the phone. Once our student understood the company protocols for answering the phone, she was fine.

Don't hesitate to call the internship provider a day or two before you start and inquire about a dress code. Ask your new boss about details on appearance and dress. Tell your boss that you are looking forward to starting your internship and would like to know if there is a dress code; what he or she expects you to wear on the job. There is much more on internship expectations in Chapter 6.

Don't Be Hard on Yourself but Always Act Ethically

Set high standards for yourself but don't set unrealistic standards. Be good but don't be hard on yourself. As an intern this means being the best you can be but keep in mind that you are primarily there to learn so you are going to make some mistakes and it is from those mistakes that you will become more knowledgeable, more efficient, and wiser.

---

[5] One "trick" I used as a young auditor in a commercial bank was to get very familiar with the written policies and procedures of any department for which we were conducting an audit. It was a key element (the review of policies and procedures) of prior audit preparation and so I learned a great deal about the work flow of a department. In addition, if I understood and was familiar with the written guidelines of a department, I could spot instances of when policies and procedures were not being followed. Who can argue with the finding: "you are not following your own written policies and procedures." As you can deduce, I wasn't always popular with my auditees!

There may be times when you feel pressure to produce at a high output. Keep in mind that quality is better than quantity. Focus on doing the work right the first time. If you feel that time or other pressures are forcing you to compromise quality, discuss the situation with your supervisor and if you are earning credit for the internship, talk about the situation with the internship professor.

Act ethically always and understand the standards of conduct for your particular internship. Ethics is one of the hottest topics in business education. That has been the case since the early 1980s and will remain the case for years to come. In all our business courses, including the internship course, ethics is woven into the curriculum and our business internship course is no exception. Unethical behavior is of great concern to business people so make sure you understand how to resolve ethical dilemmas as you confront them. If your company has standards of ethical conduct, review them early on and ask your supervisor questions. If your company doesn't have standards in writing, it is fine to trust your moral compass but as an additional step, you may want to read the ethical standards of an organization in the same line of business as your internship provider. In fact, that is exactly what we ask our interns to do if their firm doesn't have a published set of ethical standards.

Be very careful about how you discuss your internship with your peers and use great discretion when referring to your internship organization online through resources such as Facebook, Twitter, and blogs. One of our interns, a young man who was not happy with his internship made derogatory comments on Facebook about his internship provider (a bank) and his supervisor (the controller). Another student read the comments and reported them to the controller who refused to prepare a formal work evaluation (a requirement of our program.) If you don't have positive comments about your internship, keep your comments off the web.

Keep in mind that employers are using Facebook (and LinkedIn)to gather information about potential full-time employees. That fact alone should motivate you to keep your Facebook and Twitter up to professional standards. Don't use the social network to give yourself a black eye. Here's some very important tips based on lots of feedback I have from employers:

- Don't post inappropriate pictures of any kind. Certainly do not post anything vulgar. It may go without saying, but prospective employers, internship mentors, internship professors (or directors) or clients don't want to see pictures of you chugging a bottle of wine or dressed up for a night at the bar. I have seen pictures of my Facebook internship page "friends" drinking and partying heavily when away at their summer or international internships. That stuff bothers me; think about how annoyed an employer might become. If you wouldn't want grandma or grandpa to see the photo or read the comment, then keep it off Facebook or Twitter.

- It is a no-no to complain about your current internship or past internships on Facebook or Twitter. We have all had complaints about jobs but there is a right way and a wrong way to handle it and a public airing of your negative comments is the wrong way. Entering a review on a service like InternshipKing.com is fine, but just be certain you are fair and keep the comments anonymous. Comments such as how much you hate your office or how incompetent your boss is could seem to be an innocent status update but it could come back to haunt you. One of our internships almost blew-up completely at semester end because of negative comments on Facebook by a student. That student risked the cost of tuition and fees (about $1,200) and the time and effort (at least 135 hours) that went into an otherwise solid internship. While everyone complains about work sometimes, doing so in a public forum where it can be found by others is not the best career move. It's not the kind of impression that sits well with a potential boss or client.

- Avoid all posting statuses that you wouldn't want your boss to see. Call me old fashion but I don't want to be associated with Facebook "friends" or Tweets that are vulgar and inappropriate. I delete "friends" that put vulgar and inappropriate things up on Facebook. Stupid postings and Tweets can cause problems. Ferris (*Ferris Bueller's Day Off*)⁶ may be able to get away with skipping school and attending a Cubs game at Wrigley, but you'll probably get hurt with comments like: "I'm calling in sick tomorrow so I can get drunk on a Wednesday." Asinine comments like:"I'm watching the gold medal hockey game online at my desk", should be avoided like the plague. Any kind of status that implies you are unreliable, deceitful, and basically anything that doesn't make you look like professional, can seriously undermine your chances at

---

[6] Ferris Bueller's Day Off was a 1986 film comedy in which the movie's main character , Ferris Bueller who is played by Matthew Broderick, takes a day off from high school to roam around Chicago with a couple of friends. They do some high profile activities such attend a Cubs game and appear in a parade, all of which today would probably have been accompanied by status updates to Facebook and tweets on Twitter.

landing a solid internship, getting a great evaluation or future reference, or landing your ideal full-time job.

Exit Strategy

Think about your "exit strategy". If this works out to be a good experience, will you look for a full-time job with the intern employer? Will you provide a copy of your internship term paper to your supervisor? What feedback can you give the employer to improve the internship? Will you show your appreciation in some way when the internship concludes? I advise my interns to send thank you letters to supervisors/mentors. Should you get a letter of recommendation from your supervisor/mentor? I suggest that you at least ask if you can use your supervisor as a reference when applying for a full-time job.

Think about keeping notes, a journal (like a diary) and/or compiling a portfolio for your internship. Although none of these methods of documenting the experience is required in our internship course (although I do require a brief work journal), each can:

- Help you learn and reflect on the experience.
- Provide content for your final paper (Internship course).

An internship portfolio can tell a complete story about your internship experience. To compile a portfolio you should get permission to keep copies of work samples (reports, emails, letters brochures, etc.) created in the course of your internship and other pertinent documents such as learning goals, job descriptions, project descriptions, and evaluations. There is much more on the concept of an internship portfolio in Chapter 9 of this book.

Checklist: Making the most of your internship

✓ Take tours, field trips, attend meetings and seminars offered by the internship employer/provider

✓ Ask lots of questions

✓ Bring questions to your internship class for discussion. Use the internship professor as a resource

✓ Be clear about what is expected of you

✓ Follow company rules as to dress, conduct, punctuality, adherence to policies, etc.

- ✓ Keep in mind that quality is better than quantity
- ✓ Always act ethically
- ✓ Develop your "exit strategy"

Chapter 6

Employer's Responsibilities and Expectations

EMPLOYERS (INTERNSHIP PROVIDERS) SERVE AN IMPORTANT ROLE in internships – particularly when the student is earning credit for the experience. Internships are a great way for an outside entity to partner with a college or university and to make a difference in the education of a business undergraduate. This type of partnership can help meet real business needs and offer a junior or a senior business student exposure to a professional work environment. Internships are an outreach activity of a college or university that offers opportunities to apply theory to everyday business challenges. Additionally, internships can be a piston in the economic development engine of a college or university.

The internship employer/provider assures that the experience is beneficial to the student and worthy of college credit. Significant opportunities for development, learning, and networking must be provided by the employer or the internship becomes nothing more than a part-time job. Employers must realize that an intern usually requires a bit more hand-holding than a typical employee. They do need to be "shown the way."

An internship employer must understand that the experience must consist of a curriculum of professional development and on-the-job learning. The professional development can include both supervised training and on-the-job learning experiences. The on-the-job experiences can include showing the intern how to perform everyday tasks and duties, the completion of special projects, company tours, job shadowing, field trips, and attendance at company training seminars.

At my college, we look for a significant element of training within the internship. We discourage internships where the employer is looking to the intern to provide services without much training. I often tell prospective internship providers that our students are not "consultants".

Student interns need to learn. We want to see new learning - learning that is rigorous enough to substantiate three credits.

Prior to my approval of an internship-for-credit, I want the internship providers to demonstrate that the proposed internship involves lots of learning. One way to do this is by making a list of learning objectives to be accomplished during the internship. I recommend that setting learning objectives be done as an exercise between the student and the supervisor/mentor.

The student must be ready to accept just about any assignment that contributes to the achievement of the mission of the department or organization. Be eager, but don't be too pushy as there is a fine line between being too eager to help and coming across as a pest. You want to be helpful and you want people to know that you want to be helpful but like anything else, don't overdo it.

Although you may have many fresh ideas and some very valuable lessons that you can bring into the internship from your classroom experiences, don't plan to change things dramatically. You are not on board to show what is wrong with the organization. Listen and learn and your input and ideas will be valued when your opinion is asked and when you become part of the team – and that may take some time.

Please don't misinterpret me. I am not downplaying the potential that each intern can be an agent of change and a source of fresh ideas, in fact, many internship providers look for that. However, unless you are asked to bring about change and bring forth new ideas, don't do so. Just carry out the tasks and responsibilities assigned to you as an intern.

What You Should Expect From Your Internship Provider

Student interns have expectations of employers. I believe that just about all students want a solid learning experience and expect constructive feedback. At the same time students want a supervisor who is not only knowledgeable, but also professional. This not only means that intern supervisors need to be extremely capable, well educated, and experienced, but they must have the ability to teach — providing detailed explanations regarding assigned tasks, being available for face-to-face consultation and meetings, and meeting frequently with students to provide feedback on the quality of the work produced.

I am often asked by employers what they can do to launch a great internship. I believe it starts with effective internship supervisors. A critical question to be answered by any employer offering an internship is:

"who will supervise the interns?" The direct-report relationship an intern has with the organization's manager is critical to determining the overall outcome of the internship's success, and the likelihood the intern will leave the organization with a valuable experience.

What the Employer/Provider Expects from the Student

It is very clear – employers want interns that display a winning attitude, are interested and engaged in the work, are flexible and available to meet work schedules, and carry out their duties till the end of the day and until the end of the internship experience. Employers want you to be serious about your engagement and to keep your negative observations private, and certainly not part of the social network (Twitter and Facebook.)

Winning Attitude

To begin with, most employers want a winning attitude. Your positive attitude that emanates from your willingness to help in any way possible will not only enhance your reputation but will afford you more opportunities to learn and achieve than interns with negative attitudes. Act as though you are always willing to help win the day.

To have a winning attitude you must develop some passion for what you are doing. Successful people have a driving force, an energy of sorts that sets them apart from others.

Interns with a winning attitude are positive thinkers. I once saw this quote which I think is appropriate here:

They can because they think they can

-Virgil.

You must believe in yourself even in the midst of failures. Have you ever read this about Abraham Lincoln?

- Failed in business at age 31

- Was defeated in a legislative race at age 32

- Failed again in business at age 34

- Overcame death of sweetheart at age 35

- Had a nervous breakdown at age 36

- Lost an election at age 38

- Lost a congressional race at age 43

- Lost a congressional race at age 46

- Lost a congressional race at age 48

- Lost a Senatorial race at age 55

- Failed to become Vice President at age 56

- Lost a Senatorial race at age 58

- Was elected President of the United States at age 60

Interested and Engaged

Employers also like to see that you are interested and engaged. You need to have unique interests in the internship employer and the profession and or industry in which you are working. Accounting firms want students who have an interest in public accounting, manufacturers want operations management students, and insurance companies want students who are interested in selling financial products. But it is more than simply matching your major with the functional demands of your internship. You must show that you have a thirst for knowledge and a curiosity that is almost unquenchable. Don't be afraid to ask questions. Find ways to demonstrate your curiosity about the organization and the industry.

You can show interest in your internship provider from the start by studying the company before your interview. Visit the web site, read the annual report, Google recent news stories and show your interest by asking good questions during the interview and each day that you work at the internship. I call this discovery process: "internship due diligence" - a phrase that I am stealing, in part at least, from the investment banking and personal financial planning world. I recently completed an assignment for a wealthy retired CEO who wanted me to study a particular Chinese corporation that he had invested in. The due diligence involved reading all I could find about the company. I read filings that company had made with the SEC (i.e., 10Ks and 10Qs), investment analysis reports by providers like Morningstar, articles in such publications as BusinessWeek and the Wall Street Journal, commentaries by investment bloggers, and annual reports and content on the company's own web site. When you have an interest in a company with regards to an internship, research it as if you were a prospective investor and absorb as much information as possible. Do this before the interview and throughout your engagement. It will benefit you in a variety of ways.

It is quite acceptable to use the Internet while you are on your internship to learn as much as you can about the organization. For example, if you have time in your first week to learn more about the organization, you should poke around the website, Google the company, read articles about the company, review PowerPoint presentations, annual reports etc. to give you valuable background. But don't use the net to check your personal email or web surf for personal reasons.

You will be bored at times on your internship and some employers may let you do homework or some other activity during downtime, but absent of such arrangements, downtime should be put to good use. Walk around and introduce yourself to people you haven't met. Perform duties that at least make you look like you are on task and motivated. Finally, do not use your cell phone or iPod while on the job.

Be Available

One expectation that many new interns don't perceive is availability. Your internship employer will expect that you will be available a certain number of hours a week and although many internship sponsors will offer flexible hours, many will not. Because of business demands, many internship companies will expect that you will be available on certain days and between certain hours.

You should understand that need because even though the internship is much to do about your learning, you are also part of the value chain of the organization and it may just be that certain days and within certain hours you will be needed to perform your tasks and duties. The show must go on and to get into the game you need to be there when the game is being played.

Although many internship providers are flexible even the most flexible want the semblance of an established schedule because they have business needs that must be fulfilled. One intern employer that I work with is flexible on the days that the student works but wants at least a few hours, three days a week and at least 10-15 hours per week. There is work that needs to be done by the intern and the company wants to be able to count on a certain amount of work engagement per week.

Some employers want interns to be available during school vacations. We have many very capable and attractive intern candidates that miss out on good opportunities because they plan on going south for spring break or home for the month we have off during the holidays. That's fine. College students need vacations and breaks just like everyone else but keep in mind that your availability, during vacations and the winter break, might have an impact on landing the internship or on your performance evaluation because availability is one of the important expectations that employers put a heavy weight on. We have one local internship provider who is not interested in internship candidates unless they are available during school vacations. The good news is that this internship is a paid one so students can earn extra money during vacations by meeting a basic need of the internship employer - the need of availability during school breaks.

Start it off Right

Make the best impression right from the start. Arrive early on the first day – at least 15 minutes early. Until you understand the "dress code", make sure you wear appropriate business attire the first day. It is always better to overdress and learn the rules than to show up in attire that is inappropriate for your new work environment.

Observe your co-workers carefully and model your behavior so as to fit in seamlessly. When introduced to new people, do your best to remember their names. That is tough at first but you must make a serious attempt to remember names. Begin by making a commitment – a conscious decision – to remember people's names. That effort alone will help.

You can remember names if you want to and if you work at it. I find that I must work hard at remembering names. For me, immediate repetition helps. After being introduced, use the person's name immediately and use it over and over – almost obsessively and that will seal it in your memory. Also, if in the introduction you don't quite catch the name, ask for it again. Then say it immediately, which will help you remember it when they walk away. There are other memory tricks for remembering names and if you find you are having trouble you might want to read more memory tips on the Internet, but whatever it takes, remember names and use people's names in your discussions and your emails. People appreciate it when you remember their names and it helps you to make your best impression.

Don't Leave Early - Ever!

From day one, don't leave early - ever! Stay at least until your end time. Leaving early looks like you are skipping out on responsibilities. Many internship employers have mentioned the "skipping out" phenomenon as a very annoying intern behavior. It is quite common for employees to be fired as a result of leaving early. Such behavior is considered a serious misconduct. Granted, there are reasons why you might have to make a request, from time-to-time, to alter your schedule. Perhaps you have a family event to go to or must have time off for a funeral or wedding. However, if you chronically ask for time off, you won't be engaged on the internship enough to meet your goals and the goals of the employer so minimize the number of requests to alter either your start time or end time. Be there a few minutes before the start time and stay at least until the end of the day.

A typical internship is about 10-15 weeks (semester long) and so you don't have a lot of time to impress your supervisor and to meet expectations, so try to hit the ground running. It is also never too early to think about your "exit strategy". If this works out to be a good experience, will you look for a full-time job with the intern employer? Will you provide a copy of your paper to your supervisor? What feedback can you give the employer to improve the internship? Send thank you letters to your supervisor/mentor. Should you get a letter of recommendation from your supervisor/mentor?

Think Business Etiquette

The College of St. Rose has a list of business etiquette items that each of its student interns are expected to fulfill when they carry out their assignments. Here is a summary[7]:

ATTIRE. Students should always dress appropriately for the work environment. The first impression is important so you may want to error on the side of overdressing on the first day. After that, your judgment should be based on the dress of your immediate coworkers and supervisors or a published dress code.

ATTENDANCE. Understand your schedule. Know what times you're expected to arrive and leave. Come in approximately ten minutes early. Always arrive to meetings a few minutes early. Always stay until quitting time. Never leave early without permission.

ENTHUSIASM. One of my student interns started at a CPA firm and was asked to cover for the receptionist. One of the partners called the office and my student answered the phone in a very unenthusiastic voice. She was told she needed some additional training, a script, and some bounce to her voice.

---

[7] The Saint Rose Chronicle, Intern etiquette: Turning credit hours into paid hours

Simple things students can do to reach success , Kyle Griffin (no relation), http://media.www.strosechronicle.com/media/storage/paper1113/news/2008/04/02/Entertainment/Intern.Etiquette.Turning.Credit.Hours.Into.Paid.Hours-3296045.shtml

Coming to work with a good attitude and a smile on your face is important. Showing a desire to learn and going the extra mile is equally important. Do your work with energy and enthusiasm. That is what is expected in most organizations.

GOOD MANNERS. Be polite at all times. Say please and thank you. Show appreciation all the time. Don't ever be rude. Wait your turn to talk and never criticize the organization. Learn how to write emails that reflect good manners.

Checklist: Responsibilities and Expectations

✓ Make a good first impression

✓ Employers/internship providers need to provide solid learning opportunities

✓ Employers/internship providers need to provide close supervision, frequent face-to-face meetings, and clear explanations regarding tasks and duties

✓ Interns must be eager to help, interested, and engaged

✓ Be flexible and available to work

✓ Work up until it is time to leave

Chapter 7

Internship Learning and Documentation

ALTHOUGH YOU SHOULD STRIVE to make the internship experience a win-win situation (a win for both you and the employer), keep in mind that you are primarily there to learn. Being a strong contributor will take time and is a worthy goal but start out by trying to learn as much as you can. You should also develop proof of your learning which is referred to as documenting your internship.

With learning as your primary goal, keep these pieces of learning advice in mind:

1. **BE ON THE LOOKOUT FOR LEARNING.** Take advantage of every learning opportunity. Take tours, field trips, attend meetings and seminars. If you are not busy with assigned work, read the company web site and review internal documents such as a policy manual or standards of ethical conduct. Some students tell me they didn't learn enough because they were left idle too often. Idle time is prime learning time. Be creative in your search for knowledge and practical wisdom. Think of the internship work environment as your business-learning laboratory.

2. **BE INQUISITIVE AND CURIOUS ABOUT EVERYTHING.** If you see or hear something you don't understand, ask questions. That's the way to learn. No question is dumb.

3. **LET IT BE KNOWN THAT YOU ARE A LEARNER.** Be open about how much you want to learn. If you are open about how much you need to learn, your internship will be much more beneficial than if you feign your knowledge. Interns are not expected to know everything and therefore you can use your ignorance and vulnerability to your advantage.

4. **BRING QUESTIONS TO CLASS FOR DISCUSSION.** Some internships are directly tied to internship courses. At the Charlton College of Business, our students earn internship credit by completing an online, semester-long internship course. The course requires online discussions, chat sessions, and written assignments. Students can ask questions of other students or the professor via our online discussion groups or direct email. Use the internship professor as a resource and don't hesitate to discuss internship questions with your faculty advisor. The Charlton College of Business, like many business schools, assigns a slate of business majors to each faculty member who must provide advising services such as assistance with course schedules and career planning advice. Your school may have the same setup or have an advising center that you can tap into.

Document Your Internship

Proof of learning is important in an internship. The proof is up to the student, in other words students should look for ways to document their internship learning experiences. There are a number of possibilities.

Think about keeping notes, a journal (like a diary) and/or compiling a portfolio for your internship – something that will serve as a scrapbook of your experience. You need a way to capture the events, activities, and memories of your internship. Those information items become the content of cover letters, résumés, and job interviews when you launch your career and begin looking for full-time work. Our online internship class requires that students file weekly work journals that provide the details of the completion of daily internship tasks.

Documenting the experience can also help you learn more by reflecting on the experience and can provide content for your final paper, if one is required by your college for internship credit. Writing a paper from documents that you prepare concurrent with the activities of the internship, provide richer, more insightful and relevant content for a paper.

Some students create an internship portfolio, an electronic collection of work products, work journals, PowerPoint presentations, worksheets, and other documents that tell a complete story about your internship experience. Some college career services departments have software that helps students prepare digital portfolios, which can be stored with résumés so that prospective employers can access when considering a job or internship candidate. There are more details about internship portfolios in Chapter 9 of this book.

I believe the documenting of an internship should start even before the internship begins. Documenting the expectations can be the first step. The first thing you need to do after landing an internship is to make an appointment with your sponsor-to-be (your supervisor) and review expectations including:

The length of the internship. For our program, the length of the internship is 15 weeks; that's in line with the length of our semester. In addition, we require a minimum of 135 hours of field experience (which averages about 9 hours per week).

Work schedule. What days will you work? Is the schedule flexible? Will they work around critical demands you might have a school like club meetings, study groups, group projects, and special lectures?

Compensation. What will be the compensation if any? Some internships are not paid. Can you afford to have an unpaid internship? Many of the students at my college want paid internships and many cannot afford to work an extra 10-20 hours per week for free. However, sometimes excellent internships are unpaid and students will make the sacrifice for the valuable learning opportunity and powerful résumé entry. During economic downturns – such as recessions - organizations may rely even more heavily on interns but may refuse to pay. Also, large companies that typically pay interns may cut back on their internship program during tough times. That might make it possible for smaller businesses and nonprofit organizations to tap into a larger pool of interns – making the process competitive for all parties involved.

Whether it is good times or tough times, many nonprofits such as hospitals, museums, and social services agencies cannot afford to pay interns or may even have policies that prohibit paying interns. The largest employer in our region is a hospital and health care group that has a policy that requires that interns work pro-bono (for free) but does offer a variety of excellent opportunities in a number of functional business areas.

Our interns that are working for profit-seeking companies generally do get paid. Students working for CPA firms, financial service providers, investment management firms, and transportation and shipping companies pay our interns a few dollars per hour above the minimum wage, making the internship a good part-time job that has the best of both worlds – learning and compensation.

Job duties and Responsibilities. Know exactly what is expected of you. You should receive a written job description. In our internship course, we ask our students to write a job description in consultation with their supervisor. We also suggest that our students get a good handle on professional expectations – including dress code, code of ethics, privacy issues, issues involving adherence to polices such as punctuality, work engagement, and lunch and rest breaks.

Evaluation. Make sure you understand how you will be evaluated. Our students must have their supervisors complete and evaluation form at the conclusion of the internship. Some students find it helpful to get a mid-term evaluation. If you think that might help you stay on track and be successful in your internship, consider asking for a mid-term evaluation.

Final Paper and an Internship Portfolio

Another effective means to document the learning of an internship is through a term or final paper. Chapter 10 details the content and suggested outline of the final paper that I require our students to write. Other internship programs require an internship portfolio. For example, the Washington Center's internship program requires all its students to prepare an internship portfolio that documents the semester long internships completed in the Washington DC area. I have reviewed several of these internships and they are so well done that no one can dispute that an excellent learning experience has taken place. The concept of an internship portfolio is covered in detail in Chapter 9.

Checklist: Learning and Documentation

✓ Document the internship at the start, during, and at the conclusion.

✓ A well written term papers or well designed internship portfolio, gives evidence to learning and shows the achievement of learning objectives.

Chapter 8

Setting Internship Goals

AT THE CHARLTON COLLEGE OF BUSINESS, we ask our students to set internship goals as they start the internship. We want these personal standards in place early and prominent in the mind of the intern throughout the entire experience. At the end of the internship, we ask that our interns reflect upon goal achievement, conducting a sort of post-game wrap-up, within the context of a term paper.

Put it in Writing

Even if your internship program doesn't require written goals, I strongly suggest that all students put their goals in writing. It has been well documented that written goals are powerful; they drastically increase the odds of success. The process of contemplating what is most important to you as far as internship objectives, prioritizing those objectives and reviewing them often, causes you to work persistently, both consciously and subconsciously, toward goal achievement. I once read about a study conducted at Yale University in the 1950s. The study showed that the 3% of Yale graduates who had written goals had more wealth years later than the other 97% of the class combined. There is something to putting goals down on paper.

Written goals clarify thinking, help you evaluate potential, and reinforce commitment. Almost religiously and obsessively, successful people write goals, keep them visible and review them daily.

When I think of goal setting I think of one of my first accomplishments as a young man - building my own home. When I was fresh out of college, in my early twenties, I wanted to build my own home. At first, that goal seemed remote. I had never owned anything more expensive than a used car, but once I wrote down my goal, set a due date, and determined what I could afford I went ahead and purchased a parcel of land. I went ahead and talked to a banker and determined how much I could borrow from my bank. With that in mind, my goal was to find a contractor who could execute the plan – a set of blue prints that I purchased for the type of home I wanted. It all worked out and roughly a year from the time I set the goal, I was living in a brand new home.

The goals and the subsequent plan are key to accomplishment. You wouldn't travel great distances without a GPS or at least printed directions from MapQuest. An architect would not think of proposing a building project without a blueprint. A commercial pilot always has a flight plan. Movie producers cannot begin filming without a script and story boards. Why? Because the blueprint and these other examples (GPS, flight plans, scripts, and story boards) are all "roadmaps" that help people to achieve the results that they want to create.

Written goals bring about commitment which is a first step towards accomplishment. W.H. Murray, a famous mountaineer who said the following, a quote I find very powerful and applicable to career goal setting:

> *Until one is committed, there is hesitancy, the chance to draw back, always ineffectiveness. Concerning all acts of initiative (and creation), there is one elementary truth the ignorance of which kills countless ideas and splendid plans: that the moment one definitely commits oneself, the providence moves too. A whole stream of events issues from the decision, raising in one's favor all manner of unforeseen incidents, meetings and material assistance, which no man could have dreamt would have come his way. I learned a deep respect for one of Goethe's couplets:*
>
> > *Whatever you can do or dream you can, begin it.*
> >
> > *Boldness has genius, power and magic in it![8]*

Without these plans, the process would be far less efficient, and probably unsuccessful. The same holds true for written goals. You need them to help guide the successful execution of your plan.

As you write your goals, ask yourself these very important questions:

---

[8] *The Scottish Himalayan Expedition* by W.H Murray (1951)

- What do I want to learn from my internship (learning objectives)?
- What new skills and knowledge do I hope to gain?
- Will this internship help me prepare for a career?
- What have I learned in my courses that you can apply to the internship?
- How will it prepare me for a career?
- How will these goals be accomplished?
- How will they (goals) be measured?

Give considerable thought to what goals you want to accomplish during your internship. Your goals will help you to make the most from the experience and bridge the gap between academic theory and professional application.

Learn How to Set Goals

In effect you will have to do some research on goal setting and clearly articulate your goals for the internship. There are many resources on the Internet that can give you background on goal setting. I ask my student interns to visit www.mindtools.com. They are also told that they can visit our counseling center for information on goal setting.

Keep in mind that your internship goals will help you define what you will get out of the internship. Make sure that you not only identify your goals but also explain how you will go about achieving the goals. Don't be superficial, vague, or too general with your goals as you will never be successful unless you create precise targets for your aim.

Here are some tips for good goal setting from Mindtools.com:

- State each goal as a positive statement.

- Be precise: Set a precise goal, putting in dates, times and amounts so that you can measure achievement.

- Set priorities: When you have several goals, give each a priority.

- Write goals down: This crystallizes them and gives them more force.

- Keep operational goals small: Keep the low-level goals you are working towards small and achievable. If a goal is too large, then it can seem that you are not making progress towards it. Keeping goals small and incremental gives more opportunities for reward.

- Set performance goals, not outcome goals: You should take care to set goals over which you have as much control as possible.

- Set realistic goals: It is important to set goals that you can achieve.

Checklist: Goals

✓ Write out your goals/learning objectives to be accomplished during the course of the internship.

✓ Be specific and detailed about what you want to learn by thinking in terms of SKAs - skills, knowledge and abilities gained through the internship experience.

✓ Learn how to set solid short-term goals by using the tips from mindtools.com

Chapter 9

The Internship Portfolio

AS MENTIONED IN A PREVIOUS CHAPTER, I STRONGLY RECOMMEND that students properly document the internship experience by use of a portfolio. This chapter expands on that theme with more details about internship portfolios. The use of digital portfolios has been increasing at a rapid rate and also has been capturing the attention of many business colleges. At my university, our MBA students are required to compile digital portfolios throughout their studies. In our internship program, we do not require a formal portfolio. However, we require that our students keep work journals, notes, and handouts from meetings and other forms of documentation that might help tell the story of the internship. At the conclusion of the semester, we require an internship term paper that further helps document the experience and helps us to assess learning (along with a few other assignments) and assign a grade for the course. So in some sense, the internship term paper is a type of portfolio.

Source Documents

Whether or not your school requires documentation you should consider maintaining a file of source documents – notes, work product documents that you may have had a hand in such as brochures, press releases, reports, and a work journal (much like a diary). Such source documents can trigger memories or help give the details of accomplishments that can later be documented on a résumé or explained within the context of an interview. Be careful to take copies of only those documents that are nonproprietary and not confidential. Confidential and proprietary information must not leave the files of the company. If you are not clear as to whether you can take a copy of a source document, consult with your supervisor for clarification. Protecting confidential and proprietary information gained in the course of an internship is an important ethical duty.

Purpose of a Portfolio

Portfolios are used in a variety of settings. Many colleges and universities are requiring students to keep learning portfolios throughout their academic careers. One software package used to produce learning portfolios is *Chalk & Wire*. Their web site states: "learners can create, reflect upon and showcase their best work. Academics can track learner development." That quote really captures the value of any type of learning portfolio - a tool to facilitate the process of creating, reflecting upon, and showcasing output while a professor tracks the learning that has occurred during that process.

Learning portfolios in general, are a representative or a selective collection of student's work, usually drawn from classroom assignments such as projects and reports. Other types of portfolios, such as those maintained by photographers, writers, and designers, serve as a documented record of all achievement relevant to a professional career. I have seen the impressive portfolios of students from our fine CVPA (College of Visual and Performing Arts) at the University of Massachusetts Dartmouth. CVPA students prepare awesome portfolios of artwork, graphic designs, and photographs. Portfolios may prove to be every bit as valuable an asset to you during your initial job search as the degree itself.

For interns in creative positions (i.e., advertising, graphic/web design, etc.), preparing a portfolio is a necessary part of the job search. However, for other, less-creative positions, using a portfolio in the job search is not as common.

But even in the business field, a portfolio has its place. A well done internship portfolio provides direct evidence of your related accomplishments. It provides your internship professor and potential employers with a "snapshot" of your achievements to date, the type of work you've done, and the type of employee you might be.

Although I don't require our business interns to maintain an internship portfolio, rather I have them prepare a term paper instead, I have wrestled with the idea of requiring a portfolio because I believe an internship portfolio can:

- Help you learn and reflect on the experience.

- Provide content for your final paper – if one is required by your college to earn credit.

A portfolio can tell a complete story about your internship experience and can greatly aid you when writing the internship term paper.

Think about your internship portfolio as a collection of artifacts that help document the work you have performed and the knowledge and skills you have acquired as an intern. It can help you:

- Assess your learning
- Connect your work experiences with your knowledge
- Reflect on your personal, academic, and career goals
- Provide evidence of your performance
- Document your acquisition of specific skills or knowledge
- Record your intellectual and personal growth
- Your portfolio can also provide potential employers with evidence of your work experience.
- Although not all employers want to take the time to review an entire portfolio, you may have an
- Opportunity to refer to items in your portfolio during interviews and you will probably find yourself mining your portfolio for material to incorporate into cover letters.

How to Compile the Internship Portfolio

Collect your materials in a loose-leaf notebook. You may want to use plastic sheet protectors for some of the items, especially original documents. You should also use tabbed dividers where appropriate. On the outside front cover and on the spine, display your name, semester, and internship site.

The second page should be a table of contents with page or section numbers. The third page should be a letter from your internship site supervisor, verifying that you completed the contracted hours and evaluating your performance. The fourth page begins your introductory essay which should:

- Explain why you planned this particular internship
- Describe the job or internship duties
- Describe the organization, agency, or internship site.
- Include work products such as copies of worksheet completed, brochures you helped design, projects that you completed, etc.

- Include your revised résumé, reflecting your newly completed internship

The remainder of the portfolio should include documents that tell the story of your internships. Here are some possibilities:

- Letters of recommendation from employers/college professors
- Performance reviews
- Copies of thank-you notes you have written or thank you notes received in the course of the internship
- Examples of writing: articles, papers , memos, emails etc. written during the internship
- Examples of projects completed
- Examples of presentations made during the internship
- Brochures/fliers created
- Certificate programs completed (provide a copy of the certificate)
- Web sites/pages created
- Computer program code or macros/apps written during the internship
- Excel spreadsheets/templates developed
- PowerPoint files prepared

Checklist: Internship Portfolio

✓ Keep copies of important source documents as possible content of portfolio.

✓ Get permission to make copies if there is any question of confidentiality or sensitive information.

✓ Think about what you need to give proof to your growth and leaning during the internship.

✓ Keep it all in a well organized folder and if possible maintain digital (i.e., PDF, Excel, PPT etc.) versions on your PC or flash drives.

Chapter 10

The Internship Term Paper

IN ORDER TO GAIN COLLEGE CREDIT for an internship, whether your school uses an experiential model with a faculty sponsor or requires that you complete an internship course, you will probably need to write a term paper. The purpose of the paper is to describe and discuss your internship and to demonstrate what you have learned from the experience. The paper is often the primary way that you "document" your internship – that is – the paper will detail all the significant activities, tasks, responsibilities, and training that you encountered on your internship.

Many internship programs have a prescribed outline or learning contract to follow. In our program, we ask that the students write a minimum of 10 pages (double spaced) that covers the following:

- Description of Internship
- Internship Goals
- Goal Achievement
- Type of Training You Received
- Typical Day on the Job
- What You Learned About Yourself
- What You Learned About the Organization
- Skills, Knowledge and Abilities Acquired
- Suggestions Regarding Company Improvements
- Recommend Experience to Others?
- Where This Will Lead

One of the biggest obstacles confronting the students who write the internship paper for my class is that they can't generate enough significant content to fill the 10 pages! My advice is that you keep detailed notes throughout your entire internship experience and keep files of work you have performed. You should also utilize a work journal to help you remember everything you have done on the job.

There are ample opportunities to demonstrate the learning you achieved throughout your internship. You can also use the paper to provide feedback on the quality of the internship as an aid to a professor or internship director in the future. If there is something that can be improved with regards to the internship or improvements to the operation, be sure to elaborate and use examples.

Examples are important throughout the internship paper. Don't just state that you received formal and on-the-job training. Describe in great detail the training, the materials you used, the videos you watched, the reading you did, and the workshops you attended. If most of the training was on-the-job, explain in detail how that worked. If you were required to shadow a staff member, describe what you saw, the questions you asked the answers you received, and so on.

Throughout your paper keep in mind that even though you may have had several of your own learning objectives, an important generic objective of an internship are opportunities to make you see the connection between the learning you have achieved in the classroom and through reading and the practical side of business. Another objective is getting an opportunity to try-out a job before launching into your career. I suggest you keep both objectives in mind, along with your own objectives, as you write the paper. Look for opportunities to bring out how you saw connections between theory and practice. Capture those moments on paper when you witnessed or experienced something that either confirmed your expectations about this career path or made you realize that you might want to go in a slightly different direction.

In the sections that follow, I elaborate on the suggested outline of an internship term paper and offer ideas that will help you flesh out a well documented internship paper. Keep in mind that the outline and the suggested section headings are just that – suggestions. If you believe you have a better approach or outline please use it. I offer these ideas as a starting point.

Description of Internship

In describing your internship, an excellent approach is to assume you are writing a job description. In our internship class, one of the first assignments is the preparation of an internship job description modeled after real-life job descriptions. The student is asked to read about how a job description is written and then asked to write a detailed one for the internship position. They are asked to consult with their supervisor to develop the content for an excellent internship job description. This assignment helps solidify expectations – early in the internship.

Including a well written internship job description in your term paper gives the reader (professor or internship director) a clear idea of the tasks and responsibilities that were required in your position as well as what skills and abilities were utilized during your engagement.

As you write your internship job description, it might help to think about why job descriptions are necessary for permanent positions. One reason is recruitment – so potential applicants understand the job and so that interviewers have the background they need to create interview questions and to determine if the applicant is qualified for the job. It might help to keep the recruitment idea in mind as you write. Pretend that your internship job description would be a necessary aid to the company as they try to hire another intern.

Job descriptions define the role of the intern and promote accountability so be sure to be clear and detailed about what your tasks and responsibilities were as you fulfilled your internship role.

Knowledge, skills, and abilities (KSAs) are often part of a job description. The below definitions, as defined by the U.S. Office of Personnel Management, may find these helpful as you write your internship job description:

Knowledge, Skills, and Abilities (KSA's) – the attributes required to perform a job and are generally demonstrated through qualifying service, education, or training.

Knowledge – a body of information applied directly to the performance of a function.

Skill – an observable competence to perform a learned psychomotor act.

Ability – competence to perform an observable behavior or a behavior that results in an observable product.

If you are lucky, your employer may already have a written internship job description that will help you compile your description for the term paper. Don't simply replicate the employers job description, certainly use it for "inspiration" and be sure to mention in your paper that you utilized information from the employer's job description, but write a complete and accurate description of the work you performed and the knowledge, skills, and abilities you needed to do the job.

What follows is an example job description. If you need more examples, do a Google search on the keywords: "job description" or "Example job descriptions".

EXAMPLE OF A JOB DESCRIPTION

Position: Controller

SUMMARY

Provide leadership and coordination of company financial planning, debt financing, and budget management functions. Ensure company accounting procedures conform to generally accepted accounting principles.

PRIMARY RESPONSIBILITIES

1.   Direct and coordinate company financial planning and budget management functions.

2.   Monitor and analyze monthly operating results against budget.

3.   Oversee daily operations of the finance department.

4.   Manage the preparation of the official annual report of actual revenues, transfers, and expenses.

5.   Manage the preparation of financial outlooks and financial forecasts.

6.   Ensure compliance with local, state, and federal budgetary reporting requirements.

7.   Work with department managers and corporate staff to develop five year and ten year business plans for the company.

8.   Serve on planning and policy-making committees.

9.   Serve as primary legislative liaison relative to company financial issues.

10.   Direct financial audits and provide recommendations for procedural improvements.

11.   Other duties as assigned.

KNOWLEDGE AND SKILL REQUIREMENTS

1.   Knowledge of finance, accounting, budgeting, and cost control principles including Generally Accepted Accounting Principles. Knowledge of automated financial and accounting reporting systems. Knowledge of federal and state financial regulations. Ability to analyze financial data and prepare financial reports, statements and projections. Working knowledge of short and long term budgeting and forecasting, rolling budgets, and product-line profitability analysis.

2.   Work requires professional written and verbal communication and interpersonal skills. Ability to motivate teams to produce quality materials within tight timeframes and simultaneously manage several projects. Ability to participate in and facilitate group meetings.

3.   This is normally acquired through a combination of the completion of a Masters Degree in Finance or Accounting, five to ten years of experience in a senior-level finance or accounting position, and a CPA.

Internship Goals

In our internship program, we ask that students write down their internship goals the first week.

Generally speaking, the goals of internships usually include:

- Applying business theory to actual working situations.
- Gaining new knowledge by performing tasks, working on projects, and completing other on-the-job learning experiences related to a business discipline.
- Gaining a greater degree of self-direction in the learning process.
- Testing a tentative career choice.
- Allowing an employer to test you. Keep in mind that internships are an effective recruiting tool – a way to "screen out" potential full-time employees.

Your term paper should document your internship goals which can include the generic goals listed above and your more personalized internship goals.

Goal Achievement

This section of the paper requires that the student discuss what they did to accomplish the goals set at the beginning of the internship. We ask students to be candid and describe any barriers that may have made it difficult to achieve their goals.

Type of Training You Received

I ask students to discuss the type of training that they received on-the-job. Training can take various forms. We hope that the internship experience will provide the student with a professional learning experience and should consist of both supervised training and on-the-job learning experiences. Successful internship experiences combine formal training with the assignment and execution of daily on-the-job tasks and completion of special project assignments. Students should consider tours, job shadowing, field trips, and attendance at company training seminars and workshops as formal training.

Typical Day on the Job

In this section of the paper, we require students to describe their typical day on the job. What duties were performed? What tasks are accomplished? Can you describe the normal routine? Some students write that very few days were "typical" and that every day is different. If that is truly the case, I like to see a description of a sample of two or three days of work. This section's content can be gleaned from the work journal.

What You Learned About Yourself

In the course of your internship, what did you learn about yourself? Was there something about the way you responded to new challenges that was surprising to you? Did you have fears about being thrown into new situations that you had to come to terms with? Did your people skills measure up to what you thought they were? What about the knowledge and abilities that you brought to the internship, were they sufficient enough to get the job done?

What You Learned About the Organization

Part of the value of an internship is learning how an organization carries out its mission. Make sure you understand the mission and objectives of the business or nonprofit agency. You should take the time to understand its products and services, its customers and markets, and the experience and background of its top managers. If you can, understand the history of the organization. Often, much of the background information you need for this section can be found on the company's web site and in the annual reports of the organization. If the company has an employee manual or policy guide you may be able to gather some critical background information from that source.

Skills, Knowledge and Abilities Acquired

Hopefully you leave the internship a bit smarter and with more ability and skill than when you started. Have you become more professionally polished? Do you have a better understanding of policies and procedures? Are you better at using computers and software and answering the phones? Whatever you gained from doing your internship should be documented in this section.

Suggestions Regarding Company Improvements

In the course of performing your internship, there were probably times when you thought about how a process, product, service, or activity could be improved. With your business education, background, and other experiences, you have learned about better ways of doing things. Act as a consultant and describe what you would change and how you would implement your ideas. You may want to do some research for this section. Learn about some of the state-of-the-art solutions that could solve problems for your subject company. For example, if you think the company could do a better job marketing its products and services, is CRM software the solution? If so, describe the current software solutions available and how your internship provider might benefit.

Recommend Experience to Others?

Now that you have completed many weeks on the job, would you recommend this particular internship to other students? We ask that our students be very honest and candid. If this is not a great experience, explain why. Such feedback is very valuable to internship course professors and directors. I want to hear about the successes and the failures.

Where This Will Lead

Some internships lead to full-time positions. Interns, who prove themselves as capable workers, sometimes receive job offers. Is that the case with your internship? Some students are asked back to intern for the summer or for another semester. Others leave their internships with references, offers of help finding a job, and valuable contacts. Think about where this experience will lead you. It could lead you directly into the career that you had always planned or it could lead you away from your original aspirations and towards a whole new world.

Checklist: Internship Term Paper

✓ Use an outline to write your paper that helps capture the story of your internship in a persuasive documentary

✓ Keep detailed notes throughout the experience so that content generation will be easy.

✓ Write so as to make a clear connection between classroom learning and readings and the on-the-job applications you accomplished with the internship.

✓ Summarize by speculating on where the internship will lead you.

Chapter 11

End Game of an Internship

THINK ABOUT HOW you want your internship to end. Are you interested in continuing to work for the organization on a part-time basis? Are you graduating soon and would consider working full-time for the employer? Even if you have no interested in a continuing association with the internship provider, think about how you want to conclude your tenure.

Make Career Aspirations Known

Your final weeks on the internship are just as critical as your first few weeks. Those last days are a time when you can make a final impression, gain more career related information, and get valuable feedback to help yourself improve as a business professional.

During the final couple of weeks of your internship, talk to your supervisor about your career aspirations and seek advice. Make your career goals known and if you have already communicated them effectively, take the opportunity to reaffirm them with your boss. Let him or her know what you are looking to do next. Armed with that information, your supervisor may be willing to offer you a full-time position, help you find a full-time job, another relevant part-time job, or internship.

Many students who have had successful internships through our college are offered a permanent position towards the end of their internship tenure. If a permanent position isn't possible, it might be possible for your supervisor to introduce you to people who will be invaluable in helping you achieve your career goals. For example, I have had accounting students who have successfully interned at small CPA firms and have been referred by their supervisors to other firms who were actively seeking full-time staff accountants and auditors.

Your Evaluation

As your internship winds down, set the stage for an evaluation. If your school requires one, obtain the correct evaluation form and get it into the hands of your boss well before your internship commitment concludes. Help facilitate the delivery of the completed form back to your faculty sponsor or internship director. Some schools require that the evaluation be sealed in an envelope while others will accept scanned or faxed versions. Whatever the requirements, be sure to follow the proper steps to assure that the evaluation is done on time and delivered before the deadline.

Ask that your supervisor review with you the evaluation since it can be a valuable learning tool. Keep in mind that as business professionals, we are all works-in-progress and therefore you must accept constructive criticism within the spirit of continuous improvement.

Thank You and References

Write a thank you note to your supervisor and to anyone else who has helped during your internship. Be sure to express how grateful you are for the opportunities afforded because of the internship. In return, think about asking for a letter of reference or at least ask if you can list your supervisor as a reference on your résumé or in response to a subsequent job offer. Most mentors will be more than happy to provide a reference and see it as part of their role in helping you on your way to establishing your career. Reference letters are also helpful when applying to graduate school.

Knowing When to Leave

Having had a successful internship might mean that your organization wants to keep you in a part-time job beyond the initial internship. If you like the company, that might be a very good thing. Having a good part-time job is terrific while you complete your studies or while you look for the ideal full-time position. At the same time, you might want to keep your eyes open for another good internship. Some schools limit the number of credits you can earn via an internship. My college, for example, only allows three credits for an internship. However, we still have students who will complete two or three internships before they graduate because they see internships as great learning experiences and as a way to increase their networking contacts exponentially.

Think about what will help you the most. Is it best for you to stay in a comfortable situation with limited new learning opportunities or would it be better for you to leave that environment and confront new challenges while building your résumé.

Checklist: Ending the Internship

✓ Toward the end of the internship, meet with supervisor to discuss career plans and solicit advice.

✓ Ask for an evaluation.

✓ Write thank you notes.

✓ Ask for reference letters or at least ask permission to list people as references.

✓ Leave on very good terms.

Chapter 12

Employers Can Design Winning Business Internships

THERE ARE GREAT OPPORTUNITIES for businesses and nonprofit organizations to start internship programs. Many large companies such as AT&T, Apple, Coca-Cola, PricewaterhouseCoopers, Reebok, Staples, and Disney have well-known internship programs and recognize that internships are a great way to try out and utilize talent and to recruit fulltime employees, but the value of internships should not be realized by just the large employers, Small to medium size companies can start an internship program and enjoy the win-win that such programs enviably bring.

There are a couple of ways that I have been involved in the start-up of new internship programs. Students approach me with an idea for an internship. Sometimes it is simply a local company that they would like to work for and they solicit my endorsement and eventually ask me to work with the organization to structure an internship. In other cases, I am approached by someone from within a company who has an interest in starting an internship and wants to know where to start.

Help Student Interns Clarify Their Goals

I need to ask the employer to demonstrate that the proposed internship involves enough what I call "learning rigor" to justify course credit. The work experience must provide the student with a professional learning experience and should consist of both supervised training and on-the-job learning experiences. Jobs that merely require the student to perform clerical or routine tasks are not considered internships.

I emphasize to employers that the goals of all internships must include at least the following (and certainly other worthy goals can be added):

- Applying business theory to actual working situations
- Gaining new knowledge by performing tasks, working on projects, and completing other on-the-job learning experiences related to a business discipline
- Gaining a greater degree of self-direction in the learning process
- Testing a tentative career choice

For organizations interested in offering an internship, I usually ask that they provide the following information so I can evaluate the proposed internship:

- Description of the company including the mission, location, sales and market coverage
- Web URL
- Overview of the internship objectives
- Primary duties and responsibilities
- What will the student learn from this experience?
- Job Title
- Compensation
- Academic preparation of the student required (graduate, senior, junior, courses taken, GPA, etc.)
- Skills required
- Hours of work
- Start and end dates
- Primary supervisor

At the Charlton College of Business, internships can be paid or unpaid. There is a misconception that internships must be unpaid and that the "compensation" comes in the form of the college credits. I don't assume or make any requirements based on compensation. In fact, I would rather that the employer offer some compensation, even if it is only minimum wage, as our students have significant expenses including the cost of transportation to and from work, home, and campus. Obviously there is more student demand for paid internships. However, some students are interested in unpaid internships that offer excellent learning opportunities and in many cases nonprofits can neither afford or are willing to pay an intern, but I believe that if an internship provider can afford it, the intern should be paid. I believe that paid internships are almost always more valuable than unpaid. The compensation element raises the bar. Most conscientious students want to provide value in return for pay and that extra effort pushes them along the learning curve. I know it is a generalization and may not be true in all cases, but a paid intern is a more engaged intern. The bottom line is that so many college students need the compensation to cover travel expenses, to help pay to upgrade their wardrobe, and to cover education expenses. Education expenses are often a consideration in the summer when the incremental cost of a credit internship is significantly higher than in the fall or spring semesters.

At the time that I write this chapter, it costs about $1,200 for a business student at our college to earn 3 credits for a summer internship. That's an incremental cost for the student - $1,200 more if the student could add the course to his or her fall or spring load - when the course is covered under the student's full-time tuition. Students can take up to six three credit courses in our fall or spring semester so that the incremental cost of adding a sixth course to a full-time (5 course) load is zero.

Getting a paid internship in the summer helps cover some or all of the cost of the summer internship course. Many times the only way our students can earn the three internship credits in the summer is if the company pays them.

Basic Questions to Answer

As part of my job as internship director, I must perform due diligence on all internships that come my way. I take this role very seriously. I want to do what I can to promote quality internships for our students. When I examine a proposed internship, I ask some basic questions:

- Does the proposed internship have goals that are congruent with the basic goals of a Charlton College of Business Internship?
- Is there evidence of an internship curriculum or a true willingness to develop such a curriculum (which is a combination of formal and informal training and learning opportunities)?
- Does the written job description for the internship position seem to indicate that this a professional level position involving a learning experience substantial enough to justify 3 credits (business elective)?
- Will the internship run concurrent with the semester and the required internship course? For my college, this is an important question because our internship course requirements provide

tools and techniques to monitor the progression of the internship and an evaluation of the learning experience. Therefore, it is college policy that the internship run concurrent with the semester.

- Does the internship require a minimum number of hours? At our college we look for a minimum of 9 hours per week for 15 weeks for a minimum of 135 hours for the semester. This requirement, of course, will vary from college to college but it is quite common to see a minimum of 120 to 150 hours for a three credit internship.

- Is the existing infrastructure of the prospective internship employer adequate to support an internship program? For example, is there sufficient space to work? Is there a desk, computer etc. for the intern? One proposed internship employer listed his company address as the same as a local shopping mall. Upon further investigation, I found that there was no office and that the company was being run out of a home and the meetings were held at a coffee shop (in the mall).

- Does the prospective internship employer have the time and resources to make a 15 week (semester) commitment to a student intern? This includes providing an adequate orientation, initial training, ongoing training, support, and supervision.

The last point is very important. If you are an employer looking to offer an internship, you must be willing to make a 15 week (one semester) commitment (in time, money, effort etc.) to do the job right. I tell internship providers that they cannot decide to drop the student half-way through the semester which might put the 3 credits in jeopardy and waste the student's money (if fees and tuition were paid for the credits.)

Basic Steps to Take

Employers need to take some basic steps to help assure a good internship program. Interns can be a black-hole for time and energy if not approached properly and when that happens, it is a lose/lose situation (as opposed to the ideal situation – a win/win.) With advance planning, interns can be a tremendous resource for a company or nonprofit agency.

Internships usually require staff members to step forward and agree to serve as mentors to the students. In addition, managing an internship program often requires collaboration with schools, internship partners, and other organizations. Most of the work for the internship provider is supervision and collaboration with the college.

In larger companies, an internship program is generally organized and managed by someone in the human resources department, and often specifically by the training manager if one exists. For example, we have interns working in the business functions of a local hospital and our contact person for all interns in that facility is a human resources manager. However, even in large companies where the HR people may run the program, on site supervisors and mentors are still key.

All phases of an internship program, from identifying prospective interns, application/résumé review and selection, to training and daily management of the intern, must be thoroughly planned and implemented otherwise all parties – the student, the company, and the college – will be disappointed with the results.

Below are some steps that will help you implement a quality internship program.

DEFINE THE INTERNSHIP (JOB). This is a critical first step. The best way to do this is to write a job description – just as you might do for any new position. Job descriptions define responsibilities and task to be performed. The best intern job description will be a hybrid of grunt work and challenging tasks designed to provide learning opportunities.

If an employer has never had an intern, it might be difficult at first to determine the types of tasks and responsibilities that can be effectively carried out by an intern. Internship providers can begin by making a list. Below is an example of what a bank or financial services firm might assign as tasks to an intern:

- Back office functions
- Assist business line managers with administrative tasks
- Gather local economic/demographic data
- Monitor industry news and trends
- Perform communications tasks, such as drafting and broadcasting press releases
- Create web content or perform basic webmaster functions
- Develop PowerPoint presentations
- Work on internal employee newsletters
- Help compile manuals or handbooks
- Assist in the preparation of management reports
- Compile staff or customer directories
- Manage databases
- Take meeting notes and write minutes

- Identify potential customers or advertising opportunities
- Plan and manage community events
- Identify sponsorship opportunities
- Arrange luncheon speakers
- Take photographs
- Manage award/recognition programs
- Monitor local, state and federal regulatory developments

Every one of the example tasks listed above can be a learning experience for a student and each one can incorporate skills and knowledge gained in the classroom and garnered by reading college textbooks.

FIND APPLICANTS. Your local colleges and universities are brimming with students in need of excellent experiences that might qualify for credit or at least work to boost a résumé. Most schools have a career services department whose purpose is to help students find employment, including internships. At our university, our career resource center will work with employers to post internship opportunities on a portal containing a database of open internships and jobs. In addition, in our college of business (Charlton College of Business) I send emails to our business majors letting them know about internship opportunities. I also post these opportunities to a blog (www.businessinternships.blogspot.com/)

If need be, you can also post ads on job sites like Monster.com or post it on your company web site. A service called Indeed.com scours the internet looking for internship postings and offers email alerts to subscribers – such as eager students looking to land a great internship. Indeed.com is an excellent service and I recommend the email alert feature to all the students I advise on internship/job searching.

If your company finds a good source of interns from a school, it is important to develop a healthy relationship with the individuals in charge of college internship programs. For example, at the Charlton College of Business, several CPA firms contact me each year looking for interns. I have developed relationships with the HR directors of some of these firms and work closely with them to find students that will work well in their firms. Nurturing those types of relationships pays dividends for Charlton, the students, and the employers - strengthening the internship triangle.

SCREEN CANDIDATES. If the job description is appealing enough and/or the compensation is appealing, internship providers will have several qualified applicants vying for the internship. Even though this new hire won't be the most critical person on your team, you'll want to make certain you have the right person in the job. At the Charlton College of Business, I rely heavily on employers to screen the internship candidates. I don't have the time or the resources to provide screening or match-making services. And it seems that most companies that are looking for interns are fine with that, in fact, they want to be the one to do the screening.

Some of the ways that employers screen interns is to set minimum grade point averages, minimum credits achieved (completed), and availability. For example, in the middle of tax season, our CPA firms want to make sure that interns will be able to report for work. They want students who either live in the area or who will not be going away for spring break. The same is true for internship providers who want students to work over the Christmas break.

ESTABLISH EXPECTATIONS. You'll get more out of your intern if you're very clear, from the very start, about what you expect from him or her. You want to be clear about the expected hours (knowing that a student's schedule must be somewhat flexible), the daily/weekly tasks they must perform, how the tasks are to be performed, how they should dress, to whom they directly report, how and when they should report progress to the team, and so on. Take time to put all of this on paper and schedule an introductory meeting with your new intern to give an orientation.

In our internship course at the Charlton College of Business, I ask students to write an essay on what they believe the employers expectations might be. I want to students to think and contemplate what is expected of them but I also advise employers to be very clear from the start of the internship as to what they expect from the intern.

PROVIDE ORIENTATION. Orientation is a common practice when a company hires new employees. A good orientation program can help interns feel welcome, fit in quickly, and get off to a fast start. Items to include as part of an internship orientation are the following:

- Introduction to co-workers, especially other interns
- Copy of organization chart
- Employer expectations
- Company policies that will impact the intern
- Dress code
- Tour of the facility

- Emergency procedures
- Opportunities to network
- Opportunities for formal training such as workshops, shadowing, and field trips

MANAGE THE INTERNSHIP. Regular communication with your intern is critical; making sure he or she reports progress on a regular basis is the way to go. Some type of periodic accountability reporting to be helpful to both the intern and to you. Perhaps a meeting once a week that requires the intern to report on what has been accomplished would make sense.

Paid versus Unpaid Internships

To pay or not to pay, that is the question. It is actually a question that I get asked a lot by potential internship providers. It is something that every employer must come to terms with. It has also been a controversial question that the U.S. Department of Labor has wrestled with and went on record with an answer in the form of a labor regulation.

Following a lot of negative publicity relating to unpaid internships - including young workers who were forced to sanitize door handles, clean bathrooms, make coffee and photocopies for no pay – the U.S. Department of Labor (DOL) in 2010 released a new set of standards for interns.[9]

The DOL came up with a list of six criteria to determine whether or not their unpaid position is fair. The DOL regulations state that a legal internship must be "similar to training which would be given in an educational environment" and beneficial to the intern, including close work with existing employees. For unpaid internships, workers must clearly understand the position is unpaid and also be informed that a job offer is not guaranteed.

The U.S. Fair Labor Standards Act (FLSA) defines the term "employ" very broadly as including to "suffer or permit to work." Covered and non-exempt individuals who are "suffered or permitted" to work must be compensated under the law for the services they perform for an employer. Internships in the "for-profit" private sector will most often be viewed as employment, unless the test described below relating to trainees is met. Interns in the "for-profit" private sector who qualify as employees rather

---

[9] (Source: *U.S. Department of Labor, Fact Sheet #71: Internship Programs under the Fair Labor Standards Act, April 2010.*

than trainees typically must be paid at least the minimum wage and overtime compensation for hours worked over forty in a workweek.

The Test for Unpaid Interns

The following paragraphs are taken directly from the U.S. Department of Labor regulations regarding unpaid internships. Keep in mind that this issue is this: interns must be treated fairly and if there is little educational benefit to their position, they must be paid. For example, the DOL states that if an employer uses interns as substitutes for regular workers or to augment its existing workforce during specific time periods, these interns should be paid at least the minimum wage and overtime compensation for hours worked over forty in a workweek.

There are some circumstances under which individuals who participate in "for-profit" private sector internships or training programs may do so without compensation. The Supreme Court has held that the term "suffer or permit to work" cannot be interpreted so as to make a person whose work serves only his or her own interest an employee of another who provides aid or instruction. This may apply to interns who receive training for their own educational benefit if the training meets certain criteria. The determination of whether an internship or training program meets this exclusion depends upon all of the facts and circumstances of each such program.

The following six criteria must be applied when making this determination:

1. The internship, even though it includes actual operation of the facilities of the employer, is similar to training, which would be given in an educational environment.

2. The internship experience is for the benefit of the intern.

3. The intern does not displace regular employees, but works under close supervision of existing staff.

4. The employer that provides the training derives no immediate advantage from the activities of the intern, and on occasion its operations may actually be impeded.

5. The intern is not necessarily entitled to a job at the conclusion of the internship.

6. The employer and the intern understand that the intern is not entitled to wages for the time spent in the internship.

If all of the factors listed above are met, an employment relationship does not exist under the FLSA, and the act's minimum wage and overtime provisions do not apply to the intern.

I have found that many employers who offer nonpaid internships, such as the Kraft Sports Group (owners of Gillette Stadium in Foxboro, Massachusetts and the New England Patriots or Merrill Lynch (Bank of America), are requiring that interns fill out paperwork that documents that the internship is part of a credit course or that the college or university will award credit for the experience. With brand names and reputations like the Kraft Sports Group and Merrill Lynch, many college students are eager to have the paperwork properly completed and in on time and are willing to take on an unpaid assignment through which they will earn college credit.

It seems that the more an internship program is structured around a classroom or academic experience (as opposed to the employer's actual operations), the more likely the internship will be viewed as an extension of the individual's educational experience (this often occurs where a college or university exercises oversight over the internship program and provides educational credit). At the Charlton College of Business, we have developed an online internship course that students complete concurrently with the field experience (the internship). The course syllabus requires the student to apply knowledge learned in the course to the internship and we believe that is a key criterion.

The DOL position is that the more the internship provides the individual with skills that can be used in multiple employment settings, as opposed to skills particular to one employer's operation, the more likely the intern would be viewed as receiving training and therefore we encourage formal and on-the-job training that help our students acquire an array of generic skills.

Pay the Intern if they are Benefiting Your Firm

Here's my personal appeal to internship providers. My personal opinion about paying interns is that when possible, interns should be paid. In a survey done in 2010 by Intern Bridge, it was reported that 77% of students need to work second jobs when working an unpaid internship experience. This leaves less time available for interns to focus on working for their employers, or requires students to miss out on important academic activities.

My position is that a win/win situation with internships is that the student should gain something more than experience if the employer is gaining from the talents, skills, knowledge and effort of the intern. Here's what the U.S. DOL has to say on this very subject:

If an employer uses interns as substitutes for regular workers or to augment its existing workforce during specific time periods, these interns should be paid at least the minimum wage and overtime compensation for hours worked over forty in a workweek. If the employer would have hired additional employees or required existing staff to work additional hours had the interns not performed the work, then the interns will be viewed as employees and entitled compensation under the FLSA. Conversely, if the employer is providing job shadowing opportunities that allow an intern to learn certain functions under the close and constant supervision of regular employees, but the intern performs no or minimal work, the activity is more likely to be viewed as a bona fide education experience. On the other hand, if the intern receives the same level of supervision as the employer's regular workforce, this would suggest an employment relationship, rather than training.

Almost 100% of the CPA firms that bring on our students as interns also pay them a fair wage (almost always above minimum wage). These interns are truly receiving an educational experience but they are also helping to prepare tax returns, perform bookkeeping tasks, and provide audit support. They are contributors and luckily, our CPA friends agree and pay them a decent wage.

I advocate all the time for our college interns. They are bright, eager to learn and help, and bring great value to your organization. Where possible, employers should pay and students should not be bashful about asking about the possibility of compensation. I have asked some employers why they don't pay student interns and sometimes it is an affordability issue and other times the answer is "the student never asked" or "we didn't know we could pay them". Some people debate the merits of pay versus pay and I say there should be no debate. It's very simple - students need money for tuition, fees, transportation, clothing and food. Let's help them if we can.

For more information on the United States Department of Labor's position of paid versus unpaid internships, visit:
www.dol.gov/whd/regs/compliance/whdfs71.htm

Checklist: Designing Internship Programs
✓ Help interns clarify learning objectives

- ✓ Compile basic details such as position description, responsibilities, background needed, supervisor/mentor, start and end dates, and hours required each week
- ✓ Have adequate staff to supervise and mentor and adequate resources to commit to a semester long internship
- ✓ Provide some type of orientation for new interns
- ✓ Decide on compensation – paid versus unpaid and if unpaid, review U.S. Department of Labor regulations regarding unpaid internships

Appendix 1: Resources

Other Publications

There are a number of books that might be of value to a college student searching for a great business internship. Unfortunately, these publications usually cover all types of internships and don't provide a focus on business internships. They also rarely provide information on local smaller companies and nonprofits that are looking for internships so my advice to students is to utilize these publications but also use other strategies for landing a great internship.

Vault Guide to Top Internships by Rebecca Rose, Samer Madeh, Mark Oldman and the staff of Vault.

This guide is published annually by Vault Inc. and is available through bookstores and Amazon.com. It profiles hundreds of internships and includes an annual top ten list of the best internships in America. However, the guide offers no explanation as to how the ranking is determined and many of their top internships are not business oriented. The 2010 edition of the book ranked the top ten internships as follows alphabetical order:

- Capital Fellows Programs
- Garmin International
- GE
- Google, Inc.
- INROADS, Inc.
- J.P. Morgan's Investment Bank
- KPMG
- Nickelodeon Animation Studios
- Smithsonian Institution
- Steppenwolf Theatre Company

Vault also ranks the top finance internships. Here they are for 2010:

- Goldman Sachs & Co.

- J.P. Morgan's Investment Bank

- KPMG

- Lazard

- McGladrey

- Morgan Stanley

- Northwestern Mutual Financial Network

- PricewaterhouseCoopers

- Sponsors for Educational Opportunity

- The Boston Consulting Group

Source: www.vault.com

The Best 109 Internships by Mark Oldman and Samer Hamdeh copyright 2003

This guide is published by The Princeton Review, a well respected publisher of education and college related guides. This publication provides more details than the Vault Guide (see previous section). However, it includes many non-business internships and was last published in 2003 so some of the information needs to be refreshed. It is available through bookstores and Amazon.com.

The Intern Files: How to Get, Keep, and Make the Most of Your Internship by Jamie Fedorko

This book is an easy read and includes many useful tips for interns. However, it does not provide company names and contacts to apply for internships. The book is 208 pages and was published in 2006. The author shares real life experiences on how to have a successful internship. It is very inexpensive and is available in books stores and Amazon.com.

What Color is Your Parachute by by Richard N. Bolles

A book that I first read over 25 years ago and is still relevant today when you are trying to find a suitable career path is *What Color is Your Parachute: A Practical Manual for Job-Hunters and Career-Changers*

The Last Lecture by Randy Pausch and Jeffrey Zaslow

This book was written by Dr. Randy Pausch and Jeffrey Zaslow while Dr. Pausch was aware of his terminal illness. This fine professor wanted to give students the benefit of his wisdom through the lenses of a man with just a few months to live. I strongly recommend this book to all my students and I like to utilize Dr. Pausch's Time Management lecture which is available on Youtube. Here's what the editorial from Amazon.com says about *The Last Lecture*:

> *A lot of professors give talks titled "The Last Lecture." Professors are asked to consider their demise and to ruminate on what matters most to them. And while they speak, audiences can't help but mull the same question: What wisdom would we impart to the world if we knew it was our last chance? If we had to vanish tomorrow, what would we want as our legacy?*
>
> *When Randy Pausch, a computer science professor at Carnegie Mellon, was asked to give such a lecture, he didn't have to imagine it as his last, since he had recently been diagnosed with terminal cancer. But the lecture he gave-- "Really Achieving Your Childhood Dreams"--wasn't about dying. It was about the importance of overcoming obstacles, of enabling the dreams of others, of seizing every moment (because "time is all you have...and you may find one day that you have less than you think"). It was a summation of everything Randy had come to believe. It was about living.*
>
> *In this book, Randy Pausch has combined the humor, inspiration and intelligence that made his lecture such a phenomenon and given it an indelible form. It is a book that will be shared for generations to come.*

BusinessWeek

Bloomberg BusinessWeek publishes an annual list of the Best Internships and ranks the leading programs according to data such as pay and the percentage of interns who get full-time jobs. To compile the 2009 list, BusinessWeek judged employers based on survey data from 60 career services directors around the country and a separate survey completed by each employer. They also consider how each employer fared in the annual *Best Places to Launch a Career* ranking of top U.S. entry-level employers released in September of 2009 by BusinessWeek. The top ten programs of the 2009 list were follows:

1. Deloitte
2. KPMG
3. Ernst and Young

4. Proctor and Gamble
5. PriceWaterhouseCoopers
6. Goldman Sachs
7. Target
8. UBS
9. Accenture
10. General Electric

Web Resources

Indeed.com

Indeed.com is a search engine for jobs, allowing job-seekers to find jobs posted on thousands of company career sites and job boards. One very useful feature of Indeed.com and one that I use and recommend to students is the ability to construct email alerts based on searches. Therefore, if you were looking for an internship in Boston, you can have Indeed.com send you daily email alerts showing internship postings by Boston-area employers. Many of my students have found internship via Indeed.com.

InternshipKing.com

InternshipKing.com is a relatively new web site offering feedback from students on internship providers. Major internship employers are profiled on the site and recent internship postings from these providers are available. Here's what it says on the site:

InternshipKing offers internship reviews, internship postings, and internship advice. Our goal is to celebrate internship programs and provide students the best internship resource in the world. We also want to promote and recognize world-class internship programs. We believe that internships are great ways to find student talent and allow students the chance to gain experience in a certain field.

Experience.com

Founded by Jennifer Floren who had a vision of a better way for college students to prepare career paths and hunt for jobs. Experience is the leading provider of career services for students and alumni. Over 3 million students and alumni use Experience to find unique jobs and over 100,000 employers and alumni post job and internship opportunities at experience.com. Check with your Career Resource Center or placement office to see if your school subscribes to Experience.com.

Internships.com

This portal claims to be the "world's largest internship marketplace." On one of my visits to the site, Internships.com stated that it had 40,667 internship positions from 12,700 companies located in 1,616 cities across all 50 states. For $20 per year, a student can get a premium subscription that includes such services as a résumé review and an "iCertified badge" for your Internships.com profile (a type of internship certification as a result of completing an online workshop on what is expected of interns). According to Internships.com, such a certification is attractive to prospective employers.

MindTools.com

This web site has content and nifty tools to help you set goals and manage your time. I suggest that my student interns that are having problems setting well designed goals visit MindTools.com and use their goal setting tools. MindTools suggests the SMART technique. Goals should be:
- S Specific
- M Measurable
- A Attainable
- R Relevant
- T Time-bound

Blogs and Tweets

If you are not a student at the University of Massachusetts Dartmouth or a college or university nearby, my blogs and tweets will probably not help you land a specific internship. Most of the opportunities I describe in my blog entries or the daily tweets I send out are located within a 50 mile radius of North Dartmouth, Massachusetts. However, you are welcome to visit my blogs or follow me on @bizinternship (Twitter). I maintain two blogs that disseminate information on internships. One of the blogs - www.businessinternships.blogspot.com - provides mostly postings of current open internship positions that have come to my attention either through direct contact or from my web searches. A second blog, www.internshipyak.blogspot.com, provides information, tips, and advice on how to land a business internship (college). I also post positive experiences of interns just as they have completed their assignments. By reading those comments, other students learn about good opportunities, the possible benefits of landing a great internship and sticking it out to a final positive conclusion.

Appendix 2: Designing an Internship Course

I have had other professors, high school teachers, and career planners ask me about our internship program. They want to know how we award credit, how we design our curriculum, and how we assure a high quality experience. I don't think there is an absolute right way to run an internship program. However, I do think that any good program must be carefully structured and should have control points – accountability checkpoints – that help assure a good experience.

There are many challenges to running an internship program. One big one is finding enough solid internships to meet student demand. My experience has been that even though we don't require that all our business majors complete an internship, a vast majority of our students want an internship. Therefore, it is a challenge to uncover enough great opportunities in a diversified offering of business disciplines.

Accounting internships with CPA firms are usually easier to find than internships in operations management. Marketing internships are also relatively easy to come upon while solid finance internships are not unless you are located in the heart of Boston, New York City or London. Internships with financial services firms such as insurance brokers and financial planners tend to be plentiful but are usually more about marketing than finance.

Then there is the issue of how you would assess the learning that is taking place in the internship. You do need some way to do that. We require that our students take an online internship course that runs concurrent with the internship. Therefore, if the student is working in an internship in the fall they must complete our internship course during the fall semester. We also offer spring and summer internship courses. At one time, we required a once a week, face-to-face meeting in a traditional classroom for the internship course but converted to the online version to add a higher degree of flexibility to the student's schedule. Most of our students are taking the internship course as their fifth or sixth course and they are working at least 10 hours a week on the internship and in some cases working a second part-time job to help make ends meet.

In the internship course we require a variety of assignments to help monitor the work being performed and the learning that is occurring. If you are developing an internship course or trying to upgrade an existing one, think about assignments that make sense – projects, essays, journals, term papers, etc. that help the instructor monitor the student's progress through the internship and help assess the learning.

Our course is always evolving. I add new readings and videos as I come upon them and am constantly tweaking the online content of the course. We offer the course through our eLearning facility called myCourses which is UMass Dartmouth's name for a Blackboard Learning Systems, a platform that allows educators to create e-learning solutions. This type of e-learning platform has been very successfully implemented through what is called UMASS Online, a very successful (and profitable) venture by the University of Massachusetts[10].

As of the time of this book, here are the assignments we require in the internship course:

Work Journals

Students are required to file work journals weekly. These are simply a short report of the hours worked, a description of the work performed, and the training received.

For example, if the relevant period of work was 2/4/08 – 2/22/08, you would list each date you worked, the hours you worked (i.e. 1:30 pm – 5:00 pm) and a sentence or two to describe what you did on the job.

Example:

Period: 2/4/08 – 2/23/08

2/4/08 1:30 pm – 5:00 pm

I spent the first hour in a training session entitled: "How to Handle Irate Customers" then spent the remaining time handling customer service calls.

2/3/08 2:00 pm – 5:30 pm

The first 2.5 hours of my work day involved a tour of the Taunton warehouse. The last part of the day involved job shadowing of the inventory control manager.

---

[10] UMASS Online was created in 2001 to meet the online educational needs of people locally, nationally, and internationally by offering accredited educational programs via interactive, Internet-based learning systems. For more information on UMASS Online, visit: www.umassonline.net

Internship Description

The student is asked to read about how a job description is written and then asked to write a detailed one for the internship position. They are asked to consult with their supervisor to develop the content for an excellent internship job description. This assignment helps solidify expectations.

Goal Setting

The student is required to read some basics of goal setting and to write detailed short-term and long-term goals related to the internship.

Making the Most of Your Internship

This assignment requires the student to write a few paragraphs to discuss how they plan to maximize their internship experience. They are asked to state what they will do to learn the most they can and to meet the goals they have set. Students are asked to reflect how they might be proactive in helping to assure that the intern experience will be a success. Rather than report to work and go through the motions, I ask them to think about strategies that they can effectively utilize to make the most of their internship.

Fitting in as an Intern

All students participate in a blog with at least three entries based on the following questions:

- How are you fitting in as an intern?
- Are you comfortable yet on the job?
- Has there been an adjustment period?
- Can you offer any tips on how to fit in as soon as possible?

The students are asked to review the entries in the blog made by classmates and make at least two entries in response to what classmates have written.

Dress Code

This is not a very complicated assignment but since some employers have dress codes and expect careful adherence, I ask our interns to describe the dress code at their place of work. If there is no formal dress code, I ask that they describe what they perceive to be the informal dress code. I also ask for their opinion of their company's dress code (formal or informal) and that they enter their comments in the discussion area of our site for all the students in the class to read.

Personal Mission Statement

Students are asked to write a personal mission statement. Defining your mission will have an impact on the internship and both your short-term and long-term goals. There are a few ways to learn how to write a good mission statement. In the best-selling book: *The 7 Habits of Highly Effective People*, personal mission statements are covered on pages 106 - 109. Many students have copies of that book or can get it from a local library. Students are also referred to certain web sites and notes to help them master the principles of mission statement writing.

Networking

Students are required to write a one-page essay on how they plan to maximize networking opportunities on the internship. They begin by defining networking, discussing why it is important for career development, and discussing networking strategies that they will use.

What Your Internship Provider Expects

This is a one page assignment that helps the student explore the employers' expectations. Students are asked to consider issues such as attitude, conduct, engagement on the job, availability, and adherence to policies such as dress code and professional conduct.

Business Etiquette

Students are asked to discuss the importance of business etiquette, professional attire, and professional conduct in general, to the operation of a business and specifically to their internship. They are asked to define business etiquette and to clarify its meaning and importance by using examples. This assignment attempts to disclose what is expected of the student in the workplace with regards to conduct and dress. They are asked to cite any company policies or directives received from supervisors.

Business Ethics

Our business school requires that ethics be woven throughout our curriculum and the internship course is no exception. This assignment requires the student to write in a blog to which all students have access. Blogs and discussion boards are a good way for students to share information with each other. The students are asked to reply to the following questions:

- What type of ethical standards (standards of conduct) does your internship employer have in place?

- How did you learn of these standards?

- How do they impact you on the job?

- If your employer doesn't have such standards, ask your supervisor why not?

If the employer doesn't have written ethical standards, students are asked to review (by searching the web) the ethical standards of another company. They are asked to discuss why character is important as a foundation for a highly effective workplace.

Time Management

We have always had a time management assignment in the course, but recently the assignment was changed to utilize the excellent video on Time Management delivered by the late Carnegie Mellon professor, Dr. Randy Pausch. Dr. Pausch gave a lecture on Time Management at the University of Virginia in November 2007. At the time, Pausch had only a short time to live, so his lecture has the sense of urgency about how to make use of precious time. It is a long but useful video (76 minutes). This is one of the most favorite assignments. I have received a great deal of positive feedback from interns regarding this video. Students are asked to view the video and write on the following:

- Describe how you organize your work.
- What are the strategies you use to get organized and to manage your time effectively on the job?
- What could you do to better organize your work?
- Who was Randy Pausch? Please research Randy's background by using Google.
- Please list and explain at least four good time management tips that you learned by watching the video.

Résumé Assignment

This assignment is quite simple. The students are asked to submit an up-to-date résumé including an entry for their internship experience. We encourage students to utilize our Career Resource Center for help on a résumé and to use a great tool called Optimal Résumé. This accomplishes one important objective: it forces the student to revise their résumé so that they will have an up-to-date document to use once the internship concludes and before job hunting begins.

End of Internship Assignment

This assignment requires students to watch a video on how to wrap up the internship. After watching the video, they are asked to discuss their plan (one page) on how to end the internship. We want them to think about the future and make sure they are planning to take all the right steps to end the internship correctly and to set the stage for your next career step.

Exploring Career Resources

This assignment requires that our interns visit our university Career Resources web site and review the available e-resources. Some of these resources can help them prepare a polished résumé and hunt for job opportunities. With that review accomplished, the students are asked to discuss what they have learned from these resources. This assignment is done on an interactive discussion board and students are required to not only enter their initial comments about career development e-resources and the topic of informational interviewing but to also reply to at least two entries in the discussion. This is an attempt to help educate each other on how they think the e-resources of our university Career Resource Center can help and to get all the interns to learn who to log onto these valuable systems – portals that will be critical to many when they finally engage in a search for a full-time job upon graduation.

Final Paper

The most important assignment is the final paper as it documents the entire internship experience. The paper is an evaluation of the internship experience from the student's point of view and it helps to document the experience. I require that the student write at least 10 pages – double spaced. I ask that they give me as many details and examples as necessary to fully explain and describe the internship experience and the learning that occurred. I also coach them on the importance of keeping a detailed work journal throughout the process as that (work journal) as well as some of the assignments (goal setting, job description etc.) helps provide good content for the paper.

Here is a suggested outline:

- Description of Internship
- Internship Goals
- Goal Achievement
- Type of Training You Received
- Typical Day on the Job
- What I Learned About Myself
- What I Learned About the Organization
- Skills, Knowledge and Abilities Acquired
- Suggestions Regarding Company Improvements
- Recommend Experience to Others?
- Where This Will Lead

Evaluation and Confirmation of Hours

We ask that the intern supervisor complete an evaluation form and a letter that confirms the number of hours worked. Each intern in our program must work at least 135 hours in the field. The evaluation instrument that we use is similar to what is used in industry to evaluate entry level staff. It asks the supervisor to rate the intern on such dimensions as attitude, ability to learn, initiative, quality of work, and relationships with others. It also asks the supervisor to comment on student strengths and areas of improvement.

About the Author

Michael P. Griffin is the internship director of the Charlton College of Business at the University of Massachusetts Dartmouth. He also teaches accounting. Griffin was the 2011 recipient of the UMASS Dartmouth Provost's Best Practices Award for his use of technology in the business internship course. Also in 2011, Michael received the Walter J. Cass award for excellence in teaching. Before entering the teaching profession full-time in 1987, Griffin worked for a number of financial services firms including E.F. Hutton, Fleet National Bank and Rhode Island Hospital Trust National Bank. He also worked as a federal bank examiner for the Federal Home Loan Bank system. As founder of Griffin Financial Concepts (www.griffinfinancialconcepts.com, Michael has been involved in a variety of content development projects for business textbook and software publishers. He is also a consultant on financial matters ranging from wealth management to financial model development. Griffin was formerly the Assistant Dean of the Charlton College of Business and resides in Swansea, Massachusetts with his wife and four children. He can be reached via email at mgriffin@umassd.edu

Another Book by Michael P. Griffin

Michael P. Griffin is the author of *MBA Fundamentals: Accounting and Finance*, published by Kaplan Publishing.

Book Description

How do you make sense of the accounting report or balance sheet you've just been handed? How do these reports help you to understand the company's performance? How do you use the numbers you have been given to make good business decisions in the short and long-term?

MBA Fundamentals: Accounting and Finance offers real-world accounting and finance basics that can be applied today. In the business world, we are frequently called on to review and analyze financial data. This convenient and straightforward guide offers everything you need to know about the numbers to ensure your business' growth.

- Understand the functions of accounting
- Learn how to read a financial statements, balance sheets, income statements, and more
- Analyze profit and cash flow
- Improve your forecasting and strategic-planning skills

This book is an excellent primer for anyone who wants to brush up on their accounting or for nonbusiness majors who are starting an MBA program. The book has been used by many instructors to train executives.

MBA Fundamentals: Accounting and Finance is available in many bookstores and in a number of formats including digital versions such as iBook (through the Apple iBook store), Kindle editions through Amazon.com, and Nook editions through Barnes and Noble. This book can also be order in bulk, for training purposes, through bookstores or directly through the author, Michael Griffin, mgriffin@umassd.edu.

Other Resources for Faulty and Students

Michael Griffin is the creator of two accounting study guides, published by Bar Charts (www.barcharts.com). Accounting II and Cost Accounting are laminated, 3-panel (6 page) guides offered to anyone studying accounting. These guides are available through bookstores or online.

Acknowledgements

I would like to thank all the students at the Charlton College of Business at the University of Massachusetts, who completed internships under my watch. I have learned so much from the way you have gone about landing your internships and carrying them out to their final conclusion. Many of these students have cleared big hurdles to gain their experiences and have had to show incredible perseverance. Some have travelled great distances for little or almost no pay; some have completed 10-15 hours a week in their internships while taking a full course load and holding down a part-time job, and some have had very difficult personal and family demands while the internship has been carried out.

I would also like to acknowledge the hundreds of companies and nonprofits that provided internships to our students over the past several years. Their work with our students has allowed countless students to grow professionally.

I would also like to thank Dr. Eileen Peacock and Dr. Susan Engelkemeyer, both who have served as deans of our college during my tenure as internship director. Eileen Peacock (who is now Senior Vice President and Chief Officer, Asia of AACSB International) and Susan Engelkemeyer (who is now the President of Nichols College) have been very supportive of the development of our program. Support by the administration is a key factor when launching a successful college internship program.

Thanks also, to Dr. Matthew Roy who helped me design the original Charlton College of Business internship course. At the time, Matthew was the Associate Dean of the Charlton College of Business and collaborated with me on the design of the course. We also taught an internship course for the first couple of semesters before it was converted from a lecture format to a distant learning/online model. Dr. Roy is now Assistant Provost and Director of the Center for Civic Engagement at the University of Massachusetts Dartmouth.

Finally, I would like to thank Kate E. Griffin for her editing of this book. Kate is my daughter and is an English major at the University of Massachusetts Dartmouth.